P9-CMW-569

THE LITTLE GUIDES

HERBS

THE LITTLE GUIDES

HERBS

CONSULTANT EDITOR
Geoffrey Burnie

FOG CITY PRESS

Published by Fog City Press
814 Montgomery Street
San Francisco, CA 94133 USA
Reprinted 2000 (twice), 2001 (twice), 2002 (three times), 2003

Copyright © 2000 Weldon Owen Pty Ltd

Chief Executive Officer: John Owen
President: Terry Newell
Publisher: Lynn Humphries
Managing Editor: Janine Flew
Coordinating Designer: Helen Perks
Editorial Coordinator: Kiren Thandi
Production Manager: Caroline Webber
Production Coordinator: James Blackman
Sales Manager: Emily Jahn
Vice President International Sales: Stuart Laurence

Project Editor: Klay Lamprell
Designer: Susanne Geppert
Consultant Editor: Geoffrey Burnie

All rights reserved. Unauthorized reproduction,
in any manner, is prohibited.

A catalog record for this book is available from
the Library of Congress, Washington, DC.

ISBN 1 875137 76 9

Color reproduction by Bright Arts Graphics (S) Pte Ltd
Printed by LeeFung-Asco Printers
Printed in China

A Weldon Owen Production

CONTENTS

PART ONE
GROWING HERBS

UNDERSTANDING YOUR GARDEN 10
PLANNING THE GARDEN 30
CHOOSING THE PLANTS 38
MAINTAINING HERB HEALTH 58
HARVESTING AND STORING HERBS 72

PART TWO
PLANT BY PLANT GUIDE

PLANT BY PLANT GUIDE 86

PART THREE
Using Herbs

Herb Craft 266
Medicinal Herbs 282
Herbs in the Kitchen 298

Plant Hardiness Zone Map 310
Glossary 312
Index 314
Acknowledgments 320

GROWING HERBS

UNDERSTANDING YOUR GARDEN

Learning about your local environment—including its climate, topography, sunlight and soil—is critical for success with herb gardening. The two most important natural resources to consider are your local climate and your soil. You might think there is nothing you can do to change your climate (short of moving) and this is almost true. What you can do is grow the right plants at the right time in the right place. All plants have basic requirements for temperature, moisture and light. Your gardening success depends on how well you understand these needs and the way plants interact with soil. Once you understand how the environment works to make plants grow, you'll be well rewarded.

CLIMATE

Climate is the way temperature, moisture and wind interact in a particular region to produce local weather. Most important for herb gardeners, climate influences your choice of plants. The leafy green exterior of a plant gives no hint of the complex chemical processes occurring within.

Weather patterns Before making your garden plans and selecting which herbs to grow, you should consider the normal weather patterns of your climate. Since normal weather includes the unexpected, enthusiastic gardeners need to become avid weather watchers. You'll have to monitor the weather every day in order to provide your plants with their three basic requirements: a suitable temperature range, a favorable frost-free period and an adequate supply of moisture. The growing season usually begins after the last frost of the cold season and ends when frosts begin again in the fall. If you're growing herbs for their foliage, they won't need to flower and set seed, so the frost-free period is less important.

SURVIVING EXTREMES

Borage, a hardy annual herb, tolerates light fall frosts but cannot survive the extremes of winter. Hardy perennial herbs, like tarragon, however, will survive winter in a dormant state.

Temperature range Most plants have upper and lower air-temperature preferences, and are therefore classified as cool-season, warm-season or adaptable to both. Cool-season herbs, like mustard, don't mind the cold and will continue growing even when the temperature drops as low as 40°F (4°C), but they stop growing or die during the heat of summer. Warm-season herbs, like basil, are heat-lovers and won't grow unless the temperature is 50°F (10°C) or above. Basil is very sensitive to cold and usually dies with the first cold snap in fall.

Winter herbs Hardy perennial herbs (those that live for more than two years) are cold-tolerant and will survive the extremes of winter by becoming dormant. Dormancy means that the chemical processes normally occurring inside a plant slow down and the plant is in a resting stage. Likewise, any plant which is very sensitive to heat will often become dormant in response to any high-temperature conditions.

Soil temperature You'll also want to keep soil temperature in mind when planting your seeds. Some herb seeds, like caraway and chervil, germinate best at cooler temperatures, while others, like fenugreek and nasturtiums, prefer warmer soil. Recommendations for the best time to sow each herb seed can be found in the Plant by Plant Guide beginning on page 84.

HANDY HINT
Large bodies of water like oceans and lakes influence the climate of the land nearby. Since the temperature of water rises and falls more slowly than land temperatures, bodies of water modify the air temperatures of the surrounding land.

BROADER RANGE
Herbs like sweet basil will thrive in dry and warm climates. The effect of water on adjacent land temperatures may be enough to hold late and early frosts at bay, giving you a longer growing season. This can make it possible for you to grow a wider range of herbs.

COOL TO WARM CLIMATES

Understanding your climate is the first step in helping you choose herbs that are best adapted to the conditions available in your garden. The next step is to learn about the individual herbs and their range of adaptability. Some herbs may be grown in more than one kind of climate.

Cool-climate herbs The following herbs can withstand winter temperatures commonly dropping below 10°F (–12°C): angelica, anise, anise hyssop, arnica, barberry, bearberry, bee balm, betony, birch, borage, burdock, caraway, catmint, chamomile (Roman), chervil, chicory, chives, clary, comfrey, costmary, dandelion, dill, dock, garlic, hop, goldenrod, horseradish, horsetail, hyssop, lady's bedstraw, lemon balm, lovage, marsh mallow, mugwort, mustard and nasturtium.

HARDY CHIVES

Chives do well in areas where winters are mild, but can be successfully grown in areas where winter temperatures may drop as low as –40°F (–40°C). Their adaptability makes chives a very hardy, as well as handy, herb.

INDIVIDUAL NEEDS

Horehound (pictured above left) is a moderate-climate herb; it grows best in areas with a mild winter. Hyssop (pictured above right) is a cool-climate herb; it needs a cold winter and easily tolerates temperatures well below 10°F (−12°C).

Moderate-climate herbs

These herbs prefer climates where winter temperatures do not fall below 10°F (−12°C) and warm, dry summers with cool nights. Nearly all these herbs can readily be grown in cool climates as well, but in subtropical and tropical climates many of them will not thrive. Moderate-climate herbs include agrimony, basil (sweet), bay (sweet), calendula, cascara sagrada, coriander, eucalyptus, fennel, fenugreek, feverfew, geranium (scented), germander, horehound, lavender (English), lemon verbena, marjoram, mint, oregano, orris, parsley (curled), pennyroyal, rosemary, rue, safflower, sage, thyme (garden), violet and witch hazel.

Warm-climate herbs

These herbs require tropical or subtropical climates, but some can be grown in cold climates in summer: aloe, cayenne pepper, coffee, ginger, lemongrass and the Madagascar periwinkle.

LIGHT FEEDERS

Temperature affects the health of your soil as well as the amount of nutrients your herbs will need to take from the soil. All plants need a certain amount of three major soil nutrients: nitrogen, potassium and phosphorus. Choosing light feeders, like sage and fennel (pictured below), makes it easier to maintain the health of your soil.

MOISTURE

Water makes up from 85 to 95 percent of the weight of living plants. It's not surprising that when water is lacking, a plant wilts. Wilting means the collapse of the cell structure in the leaves and stems. Your goal is to water before wilting occurs.

HAND WATERING
Watering by hand may be the only practical option for irrigating small plantings. It's also useful for settling in seedlings. Hand watering isn't ideal for established herb plants, since it usually can't supply enough water to soak slowly into the soil.

Rainfall As a general rule, your herb plants require the equivalent of 1 inch (25 mm) of rainfall each week. In some climates, snowfall contributes greatly to the annual water supply. Even though snow usually falls when most herbs are dormant, it still makes a noticeable contribution to the water reserves held in the soil below the surface. Gardens in hot, dry climates lose moisture faster and may need the equivalent of 2 inches (50 mm) each week. To monitor the rainfall in your garden, buy a rain gauge (available at most hardware stores) and set it in your garden. Check it immediately after rain, before the water in the gauge evaporates.

Checking soil moisture There are several methods of checking soil moisture. Move the surface soil or mulch and look at the soil in the root zone. Most plant roots are in the top 12 inches (30 cm) of soil. If the soil is cool and moist and there are no signs of plant stress, such as discoloration or wilting, you can probably hold off on the hose. A daily check is a good idea in dry weather. You can

---

HANDY HINT

You should water sufficiently to keep your plants growing, but not so much that the roots become starved of oxygen. One good soaking is often better than several shallow waterings because it encourages roots to spread in search of water.

---

also take a soil sample from the root zone and examine it. Dry, sandy soils will flow freely through your fingers but will stick together slightly with adequate moisture. Heavier clay soils will appear hard and crumbly when dry and feel slick when adequately moist.

Watering systems Although popular and inexpensive, overhead watering systems are based on a plentiful, even extravagant, water supply. In the time it takes water to reach the soil, 30 to 50 percent of the water used may be lost to evaporation on a hot, windy day. Trickle irrigation eliminates some of the problems encountered with overhead systems. Trickle lines use less water, since they apply water directly to the soil, where plants need it. Less water runs off and more water sinks in. Cool water helps to keep the soil temperature low, especially if you mulch. And

SOAKER HOSES
Watering is most effective at ground level. When digging to plant, lay a line for a soaker hose (which leaks droplets or sends fine sprays of moisture along its length). It will moisten the planting without benefiting the weeds nearby.

since foliage remains dry, fungal diseases are not encouraged. The disadvantage is that trickle systems require more expensive and more time-consuming installation.

EXPOSURE

The quantity and duration of light in your garden affect the growth of your herbs. The intensity of the light influences photosynthesis, the plant's internal process that employs light energy to produce carbohydrates or sugar for food, using carbon dioxide and water.

Seasonal sunlight The intensity of sunlight varies with the season, the geographic location and the atmosphere. During the winter, the Sun is lower in the sky than it is during the summer. Sunlight travels a longer distance through the atmosphere and strikes the Earth at a lower angle. As a result, it is less intense. In summer, sunlight reaches the surface more directly and is more intense.

Shade To make sure your herbs get the right amount of light, take into account shade from trees, hills

and buildings when you're planning your garden. Space plants correctly and weed regularly to reduce competition for sunlight. Some plants prefer shade, others need full sun.

Direct sunlight Plants that need full sun are able to stand uninterrupted, unfiltered sunlight from sunrise to sunset. Plants that prefer partial sun will usually be able to stand about five to six hours of direct sunlight, with shade or filtered sun the rest of the day. Place herbs

LESSENING THE LIGHT
Tall crops planted to the south or west of shorter crops will provide shade for them. Also take into account that when dust and other pollutants are in the air, less sunlight reaches your garden.

SHADE-LOVING PLANTS

Sassafras will thrive in the shade cast by taller trees. And you can grow some smaller shade-loving herbs under a sassafras. When shade-loving plants receive too much sun, leaves may wilt, or may develop a bleached appearance and grow poorly. With inadequate sunlight, plants become lanky and pale, and they flower poorly or not at all.

that do best in partial shade in filtered, indirect light where trees provide dappled shade. Few herbs need to be in full shade, but if that is the recommendation, the herbs will need just that: solid and dense shade away from all direct sun.

Light and dark The daily cycle of light and dark influences several plant functions, including seed germination, root initiation and the growth of blossoms, fruits and bulbs. In the tropics, the normal duration of sunlight is 12 hours a day. In the areas north and south of the equator, the length of day varies with the season and the latitude, until the occurrence of day-long light in summer and darkness in winter, near the Poles. Some plants require short days and longer nights to bloom and are called short-day plants. Plants that flower when the days are long and the nights short are known as long-day plants.

Long-day herbs include most annuals. Plants that are unaffected by day length are called day-neutral.

Windy conditions Your herbs will require more water under windy conditions, as wind draws away moisture released through pores faster than normal. Wind shelter is important for your more sensitive herbs.

SOIL

Good soil is the herb gardener's key to success. Besides providing physical support for plant roots, soil contains the water and nutrients plants need to survive. A good soil is loose and well drained, but it also holds enough water and air for healthy root growth.

Soil composition Soil is a mixture of mineral matter, organic matter, water and air. Soil has approximately 45 percent mineral matter, 5 percent organic matter, 25 percent water, and 25 percent air. Organic matter is an essential part of the soil makeup because it supplies nutrients to the plants and can help to improve drainage. Soils with a lot of organic matter are usually dark in color.

Soil texture Soil texture is determined by the proportions of different-sized mineral particles in the soil. Soil texture can have a great effect on the growth of your plants. Roots will spread easily in open sandy soil, but water will drain away quickly, so your plants may need more frequent watering. In a tight clay soil, roots cannot penetrate so readily and the soil will tend to become waterlogged. To check the texture of your soil, take a handful of your damp garden soil and squeeze it. If it crumbles slightly when you release your grip, its texture is probably satisfactory; if it runs through your fingers, it is too sandy; if it forms a sticky lump, it is too clayey. In general, loamy soils, which contain moderate amounts of clay, silt and sand, often suit most plants best.

Soil structure The structure of soil depends on the way the various particles—sand, silt and clay—come together to form clumps or aggregates. Most plants prefer a soil with a loose, granular structure. This type of structure has lots of open space (called pore space) that can hold air or water. The water forms a thin film around the granules and holds dissolved nutrients such as calcium and potassium. Plants can take up these nutrients when tiny hairs on the tips of their roots enter the water film between the soil particles. Adding plenty of organic matter is an effective way to promote a good soil structure. Add organic matter to your soil in the form of compost.

THE NITROGEN CYCLE
The natural cycle in rejuvenating soil is this: Animals feed on plants; animal manures add nitrogen to the soil; the plants take up nitrogen; the plants decompose and put nitrogen back into the soil. Along the way some nitrogen is lost to the air, but is returned with thunderstorms. The alternative is to add organic matter.

SOIL continued

Air and water Your plants will require a good deal of water but they must also be able to take in air (for oxygen) through their roots. Most garden plants grow best in well-drained soil. They don't like to have wet feet, since flooding cuts off the supply of oxygen to the roots. Plants obtain their oxygen from air-filled pores in the soil, and during the daytime take in carbon dioxide from the air. Oxygen they can't use is given off from their leaves during the daytime, and we take that in.

Soil nutrients The availability of soil nutrients is dependent on the interaction of many factors, including the texture and structure of the soil, the amount of moisture and organic matter, and the pH. A fine texture, a loose structure, ample moisture, high organic matter content and near neutral pH are all conditions that make the most nutrients available to your plants. One of the most important of plant nutrients is nitrogen, which is found in soil in various chemical combinations that plants can absorb. Keeping an adequate supply of nitrogen in soil can be a challenge, since nitrogen is used up very quickly by plants. It also dissolves in water and leaches out of the soil. For plants to thrive, the nitrogen must be continually replenished.

Lab check To check the nutrient content of your soil, it may be worthwhile to have a laboratory test your soil before you begin serious gardening. Even soils known to be highly fertile often

HAND TESTING
Soil should crumble lightly when squeezed. Clayey soil forms a sticky lump when it is squeezed.

lack specific nutrients or essential minerals. Private soil-testing agencies will indicate any specific needs. You can test again in a few years to monitor the results of your gardening practices and make adjustments if necessary. The testing agency will usually also recommend rates of application of fertilizing substances and lime based on the plants you've decided to grow, since crops vary in their requirements. Make sure you ask for advice on fertilizers that are organically based.

Soil pH It is helpful to know how acid or alkaline your soil is. If you have the soil tested, the results will include pH, which is the measure of acidity or alkalinity. Soil pH is important because it influences soil chemistry. Many herbs prefer a soil on the slightly acid side. Plant nursery operators

will know the approximate pH level that suits the plants they sell. Heavy, dense clay soils are often more acid than is desirable. Lime or dolomite will render them less acid and improve their structure. If your soil is too acid for the plants you plan to grow, the laboratory will be able to tell you how much lime to add. If your soil pH is high, you can lower it by adding a sphagnum peat substitute or sulfur. It's

important not to add lime or sulfur unless it has been advised for your soil.

Soil pH scale Herbs can absorb most nutrients from the soil when the soil pH is in the neutral range. The pH scale works like this:

    1–5 = strongly acidic;
    5–6 = moderately acidic;
    6–7 = slightly acidic;
    7 = neutral;
    7–8 = slightly alkaline;
    8–9 = moderately alkaline;
    9–14 = strongly alkaline.

Herbs can't absorb nitrogen, for example, if the soil pH drops much below 8, while iron is less available as the pH moves above 8.

PUZZLING OUT PH

While a lab test will give you very specific information on your soil's acidity or alkalinity, a litmus test kit is an easy and inexpensive way to get a rough idea of your soil's status.

COMPOST

Whether your garden is large or small, it's worth devoting some space to a compost pile to convert otherwise wasted products into the ultimate soil amendment. Worked into the soil or used as a mulch, compost can add nutrients and increase the water-holding capacity of dry, sandy soils.

How to start Save any organic wastes that you would normally discard, but don't use such waste products as oils and meat scraps, since they will attract scavenging animals and slow the process of decomposition. Also avoid human or pet feces, pesticides and pesticide-treated plant material, such as grass clippings from treated lawns. Don't add weeds or insect-infested or diseased plants unless you have a hot compost pile (you can learn more about hot and cold composts on page 26). It's also not a good idea to add roots

of perennial weeds in case they survive the composting process and are distributed throughout your garden as you spread your finished compost.

Compost bins Compost can be in an open pile, but bins look neater and help keep animals out of the pile. You can choose from a variety of commercially sold timber or plastic containers, or you can make your own from timber, cement blocks, bricks or chicken wire nailed to garden

---

HANDY HINT

Soil temperature has an effect on plant growth. Roots tend to grow more slowly in cool soil, so your herbs may have trouble getting nutrients for their flush of spring growth. An early spring application of compost will supply their needs.

---

stakes. If you have the space, a multi-bin system is ideal, so when one part is full, you can start filling up the other side.Whatever design you choose, stand it on a level, well-drained surface to prevent the pile from sitting in water. A coarse material, such as straw or the stalks of sunflowers, is best as the bottom layer of the heap so that air can circulate freely.

Keeping compost moist If all the green material added to your compost is relatively moist, it will not be necessary to add extra water. If materials have been allowed to dry out, you may need to moisten them for effective breakdown. By adding a few shovelfuls of good garden soil or finished compost to the pile, you will add to the microorganisms that help carry out the composting process. If the weather has been

Chicken wire lets air in.

Compost is contained.

dry and hot, each time you add new materials, such as soil and composting ingredients, sprinkle the compost pile with water. This will make sure the pile contains the moisture that is necessary for even decomposition.

Hot compost This type of compost can be ready in around two to six weeks or as soon as the temperature stabilizes and the individual materials you added at the beginning are no longer recognizable. Waste material is

25

COMPOST continued

stacked layer upon layer, or just jumbled together. Mix materials that are high in carbon with materials high in nitrogen. You can achieve a good balance with approximately equal volumes of dry materials such as leaves, straw or paper and moist green materials or manure. Too much carbon will mean the pile remains too cool. And excessive nitrogen creates odor problems. Sprinkling soil on alternate layers will inoculate the pile with the right decomposer organisms. Wherever possible, break materials down before adding them to the pile. Woody prunings, tree bark and newspaper should be shredded to fine pieces. Weeds, insect-infested or diseased materials should go in the center, where they will be exposed to the highest temperatures.

Cold compost This is a much slower process of decomposition and requires no turning over with a garden fork. After piling together

JUST ENOUGH

Too much of a nutrient like nitrogen in the soil will make plants such as nasturtiums produce leafy growth at the expense of flowers. If the plants you have now seem to be growing well, you may want to assume that the nutrient levels are fine and just apply compost in early spring.

your waste material, simply wait six to twelve months. Don't add materials contaminated with pests, since temperatures won't be hot enough to kill them off. When your compost is fully decomposed, shake it through a wire mesh to screen out large particles. Each spring, spread 2 inches (5 cm) of compost over the surface of your garden. If soil tests indicate a nutrient imbalance, fertilize the soil appropriately first, and then add the compost by digging it in or leaving it on the surface as a mulch. You can use compost indoors as a potting mix.

TREATING ODOR

If odor is a problem with your hot compost, the pile needs to be turned and aerated; if it is too wet, mix in more dry materials and cover the pile with a tarp. If the breakdown is too slow, add more green or nitrogenous material or water the pile.

MULCHING

Mulching simply means covering the surface of your garden soil with a layer of organic or inorganic material. Mulching keeps your soil warmer in winter and cooler in summer. It also helps retain soil moisture and protects soil from erosion.

Mulching tips If you are planting in early spring, wait until the soil warms up before mulching. If you are planting in the fall, apply the mulch right after planting. Mulch earlier in dry climates to trap the moisture from spring rains. In wet climates, mulch a bit later in the season to give the soil a chance to dry out.

Organic mulches Organic mulches, such as compost, grass clippings, shredded leaves, straw and hay, are a good choice for mulching, since they'll improve your soil while providing all the other benefits of a mulch. They will add organic matter and nutrients to the soil while they decompose, enhancing soil productivity. Use whatever organic materials are most easily available to you. The beneficial organisms in compost help control soilborne

KEEPING WARM
Though not as attractive as organic mulches, black plastic is very effective in helping soil retain the warmth from the Sun into the night, preventing weed growth and retaining soil moisture.

FALL MULCH

Leaves make an excellent mulch for your herb garden. Don't use the leaves unshredded, as they can blow away when dry or create an impenetrable mat when wet, preventing moisture reaching your plants' roots.

plant disease so that it won't spread as easily. There's no need to remove the mulch at the end of the season, since the compost decomposes naturally.

Shredded leaves Shredded leaves also make a nutrient-rich mulch. You can prepare them with a leaf-shredding machine or simply run over piles of leaves with a lawn mower. Straw is preferable to hay, as hay tends to carry weed seeds and provide a habitat for rodents, snails and slugs. Bark and wood chips work well to keep down weeds in plantings of perennial herbs.

It's easy to pull out any weed seedlings that do sprout up.

Inorganic mulches The most common inorganic mulching materials are black plastic and landscaping fabrics. Don't use black plastic under shrubs, as it can cause the roots to grow too close to the surface of the soil. Landscaping fabrics allow water and air to penetrate, can be walked on and look better than plastic.

29

PLANNING
THE
GARDEN

If you're planning a new herb garden, you'll need to consider your garden's location, size, shape and design. Start out simple. Seek inspiration from books and experienced gardeners. If you enjoy formal patterns, plan your garden along the lines of an Italian Renaissance garden or a knot garden, in which intertwining miniature hedges of different herbs create a knot-like shape. For something more informal, think about a cottage garden. Or perhaps you would prefer to specialize and grow a kitchen garden full of culinary herbs, or a medicinal herb garden.

HERB GARDEN SITE

First decide where to locate your herb garden. You could reassign a section of your existing vegetable or flower garden, or perhaps create a whole new garden devoted to herbs. Or you may place herbs in several different small sites.

Finding a level site To choose a site, begin with a tour of your garden. If possible, it is important to choose a level site with good drainage, since it is easier to garden on flat surfaces and soil erosion won't be a concern. You should try to avoid hills that lose moisture quickly or where the soil is compacted and therefore hard to dig. Stay away from pockets of low-lying

TOUGH SITES

If you're starting from scratch, put as much thought as you can into site selection. Clear all rocks and brush from the site before you start.

land, where poor drainage and inadequate air circulation could encourage related disease and pest problems. If you have to garden on a slope, consider planting across the slope, rather than in rows running up and down, to prevent erosion.

Site considerations An important consideration in choosing a site is access; you may only need room for a wheelbarrow to move between rows or beds, or you may need to provide access for a truck to deliver a load of soil. Try not to plant in the root zones of trees, as digging around the roots could injure the trees, and the trees will compete with your herbs for moisture and nutrients in the soil. Be sure you have access to an adequate water supply and that your plants will get full sun for most of the day.

SUITING SITE CONDITIONS

A garden site has to suit the plants you will grow. If your site is shady, choose herbs that will tolerate shade. If your site has wet conditions part of the year, choose plants that can tolerate this. If you have a range of possible sites, choose the one that provides as closely as possible the specific requirements of the plants you want to grow. An ideal site will also correspond with your ideas of what a garden should be and where it should be. It may be most convenient for you to have your herb garden located near the kitchen door. Or perhaps you'll get most enjoyment from one that may be viewed from indoors through a window.

CHOOSING WISELY

In the long term, especially if you plan to live in the same place for several years, you can avoid many problems and create a wonderful vista for your yard by choosing a good location.

GARDEN SIZE

The size of your herb garden will be determined by how much you want to grow and harvest, the suitable space available to you, the amount of time you have and the availability of resources. If you're a beginner, it may be best to start with a small garden until you gain experience.

Deciding on size One or two plants of a herb you have not grown before is usually enough to start with, but you will soon develop favorites and learn which grow well in your garden. For instance, parsley is a popular and nutritious herb with many culinary uses, so it is worthwhile to have a dozen plants at a time to ensure a good supply. A dozen basil plants would not be too many if you want to make pesto regularly.

THINKING ABOUT PATHS
Paths are a necessity for work in a large garden, and a garden stroll can also follow the paths you've planned. For both work and leisure, make garden paths 4 to 5 feet (1.2 to 1.5 m) wide. If you're planting in beds, keep them under 5 feet (1.5 m) wide, not more than twice the distance you are able to reach from the side.

PATCH PLANTING
If you have limited amounts of space, you may choose to garden in several small patches. Position plants that need daily attention or frequent picking close to the house. If space is limited, take advantage of borders along paths and fences. At the least, you can dress your windows outdoors with boxes of luscious herbs close at hand.

In the garden, a dozen parsley plants would require about 3 square feet (about 3 sq m) of space, and a dozen basil would need about 2 square feet (about 2 sq m). A large perennial like angelica, would need about 12 square feet (about 12 sq m), while a smaller shrub, like barberry, would require about 16 square feet (about 16 sq m). The guidelines on the seed packet, or in the "Plant by Plant Guide," will give you an idea how much space your herbs need.

Time requirements When deciding on the size of your herb garden, you may want to think about the time you have available to tend your garden. The time any garden needs varies with climate and season, as do the tasks to be done. You'll need to prepare the soil by digging and adding nutrients where necessary, plant your seeds or seedlings and perform regular maintenance tasks, including weeding, watering, pest control and harvesting. The work will be slower if you're using hand tools rather than powered tools.

Matching resources If soil moisture is limited, due to climate or soil type or topography, you will have to devise a way to supply water. A large garden will require more water than a small one. Mulching is an excellent way to control weeds and conserve soil moisture, but if you plan to mulch, how much material will you need? If you are starting a new garden, how much of an investment can you afford to make in soil amendments, plants, seeds, watering equipment, tools and structures during the first year? If you're unsure of the answers to these questions, keep it small and simple the first year.

GARDEN STYLE

Regardless of the size, shape or location of your garden, its style is a reflection of your own tastes. The number of possible herb-garden styles is limited only by your imagination and creativity. You can plan one or more theme gardens to concentrate on a particular aspect.

Simple shapes The simplest gardens to set out and manage are square or rectangular. If you must take advantage of every square inch of space, it makes sense that you will follow the general outline of your property, and land is most often sold in boxlike shapes. Laying out your herb garden with square or rectangular beds not only may be the most practical way, but can give the garden a formal look that appeals to many gardeners.

DESIGN FOR LARGE GARDENS
Divide a large square site by grouping herbs that serve particular purposes. Medicinal, dye, fragrance and culinary gardens are some examples. Avoid walking on beds as you work. Once you've designed the look and location of your paths, beds or rows, begin selecting and arranging your plants.

Creative shapes Of course, squares and rectangles aren't the only shapes. You may choose to lay your garden beds following the curve of a hill, stream, fence or stone wall, or design them to accent the shape of a building. If you want to be especially creative, garden within unusual boundaries like circles or ovals. You can make a garden in the shape of a spiral with one continuous bed beginning in the center and spiraling out in circles. (It is best to avoid circles and curves if you have limited space.) A book or magazine on garden landscaping will offer you examples to follow in shaping your garden beds.

Planning the design Whatever design you choose, try it out on paper first. Use graph paper and do not draw to too small a scale. For example, you can let each square of the graph paper equal a square foot (900 sq cm) of your property. Keep it simple. Mark the outline of the garden first, then add other features of the location, including existing and future trees, shrubs, fences, paths, hills and buildings. Make several photocopies of the base plan and use the copies to draw out your different design ideas. Or simply lay tracing paper over the original plan and draw on that. That way, you'll always have a fresh base plan if you want to start over.

HANDY HINT
Whatever the size or shape of your herb garden, you can add style to your design by selecting herbs that flower at the same time or share the same color. It is especially easy to create lavender and blue themes with herbs. Or focus on the foliage of your herbs and plant blue-green or silvery herbs mixed with darker greens for contrast.

PLANNED INFORMALITY
At one extreme are the formal herb gardens with their angular knots and pruned hedges, and at the other are random groupings of whatever suits the season. In between, there is the garden that appears to be meandering but is carefully planned around a particular use for the herbs or theme, such as color or fragrance.

38

GROWING HERBS
CHOOSING
THE
PLANTS

Y ou can choose herbs for your garden for their useful fruits, attractive leaves, fragrant flowers or perhaps for deep taproots that cope better with a poor water supply. If you want your herb garden to be attractive all year round with minimal work, you may want to concentrate on perennials rather than annuals and biennials. On the other hand, planting annuals will give you more flexibility. Knowing about the functions and characteristics of the various plant parts will help you identify, select and maintain your herbs most effectively.

ANNUALS

Annuals germinate, flower, set seed and die within one year. They are generally easy to grow and offer the herb grower a wide range of plant sizes, colors and shapes. In a new garden they are especially useful for filling spaces between perennials that are just newly planted.

DUAL-PURPOSE HERBS
Some annual herbs, such as coriander, can be grown either for their foliage or for their seeds.

Water regularly Whether the annuals you've chosen can be planted directly into the garden soil outdoors or need a warm start indoors, it's important to provide them with plenty of water. Most annuals have shallow roots, which means their roots remain near the surface and can dry out easily.

One per pot Annuals that need plenty of space, like basil, should be planted one per pot. If a pot contains several seedlings, you will find it difficult to separate them without damaging their root systems. Annuals that form clumps, like dill and chives, may be sown thickly in the pot.

Mixing perennials and annuals If you're confined to gardening in the shade, use the opportunity to grow as many shade-loving herbs as possible, mixing herbs with different life spans. Include angelica, chervil, lemon balm and sweet cicely. In wet areas, select from the wide

---

HANDY HINT
Annuals grow quickly from seed. So do a few short-lived perennial herbs—including fennel, plantain and vervain—so you can treat them as annuals and grow them from seed each year. This will give you the best supply of healthy foliage.

assortment of plants in the mint family. If you are going to plant annual herbs between your perennials, it's a good idea to find out about the particular requirements and growing characteristics of the perennial herbs. Some, like mint, are very invasive, and are best planted in buried containers such as clay drainage pipes. You can also use large plastic pots that are at least 12 inches (25 cm) deep and remove the base.

Easy-to-grow annuals Many annuals bloom all season and are then able to propagate themselves

DEPENDABLE BLOOMERS
Calendula, or pot marigold as it is commonly called, is an easy-to-grow annual. Its flowers, which bloom in summer, provide long-lasting color for fresh bouquets and dry well, retaining their color.

by producing lots of seeds. Some, like borage and coriander, will reseed before the end of the season and their offspring will germinate in the following season. Remember that easy-to-grow doesn't always mean easy-to-get-going. If there's no information with the seedlings you buy, ask the garden center

whether your annual seedlings need to be carefully nurtured indoors before being planted outside. Some easy-to-grow annual herbs include anise, basil (sweet), borage, calendula, cayenne pepper, chervil, coriander, dill, fennel, fenugreek, mustard, nasturtium, plantain, safflower and vervain.

BIENNIALS

Like annuals, biennial herbs are generally easy to grow. Biennials germinate, flower, set seed and die within two years. During their first year they produce plenty of foliage and strong root systems. Many biennials depend upon nutrients stored in their large roots to survive the winter.

Sowing biennials If you start biennials, like caraway and parsley, from seed indoors, sow them in peat pots that can be placed directly in the ground to avoid disturbing the sensitive taproot during transplanting. If your climate allows, sow biennials directly into the garden so you won't have to transplant them out later. This will help you avoid taproot damage. Biennials flower and make seed in their second season, just before they die.

Harvesting decisions How you grow a biennial herb depends on what you want to harvest

CARAWAY COOKING
Caraway plants are biennials that may bloom in their first or second year, which is why they are sometimes referred to as annuals.

from it. Parsley, for example, is commonly grown for its first-year foliage, not for its second-year flowers and seeds. So even though parsley is technically a biennial, you'll need to start new plants each year if you want a good supply of foliage.

Rotating herb crops Rotating your annual and biennial herb plants is a good idea, especially before you encounter any pest problems. Crop rotation, which means avoiding planting the same crop in the same place two years running, is common practice in organic gardening. If you usually grow several large annual crops, it makes sense to work out a rotation based on the same number of growing plots. The result will be that a given area will repeat a particular crop only every third or fourth year. Simply avoid planting the same herbs in the

same location each year, so that potential pests won't build up to the point of causing noticeable damage. Rotation also helps to avoid the danger of exhausting the supply of plant nutrients especially favored by particular crops.

Interplanting biennials It's easy to grow biennial herbs with annual and perennial herbs in the one garden. You can just start the annuals and biennials from seed as necessary, and use them to fill in between the longer-lived perennials. Mix leafy biennials like parsley, caraway and chicory, which are easy to grow, into perennial plantings, harvesting the foliage the first season and enjoying the flowers or seeds the second year, when the foliage will be tougher and not as plentiful.

NON-COMPETITIVE BIENNIALS
Biennial parsley is shallow-rooted so it won't compete for moisture with a deep-rooted plant. Many biennial herbs can be used in vegetable and flower gardens to complement the rooting patterns, nutrient needs and tolerance for light and shade of the other plants.

PERENNIALS

Perennial herbs live for more than two years. Some reach their prime within five years. Growth then declines, and the plants die unless they are resurrected by thinning and division. Other perennials thrive and continue spreading, unless you check their growth with judicious thinning.

Life cycles Perennial herbs form the backbone of most herb plantings. They are hardy plants that return year after year, giving structure and continuity to your herb garden. You can propagate a perennial vegetatively or from seed. Vegetative propagation involves plant division, layering or taking cuttings, and it is the easiest and the quickest way to increase your stock of perennials. The seeds of some perennials may be difficult to germinate and others, like tarragon, don't make seed at all. While most perennials started from seed will flower during their second year, new plants started vegetatively often flower in their first year. Some herbs that are normally perennial in warm climates cannot survive the winter temperatures of colder climates.

LOVELY LAVENDER
Lavender is a small, rounded perennial shrub, known and beloved for its fragrance and its herbal and ornamental qualities. It's good to shear the plants every few years to encourage fresh new growth.

Popular herbaceous herbs

Herbaceous perennials have stems that usually die back to the ground in the winter and grow again in the spring from a persistent rootstock. Popular herbaceous perennials include agrimony, aloe, angelica, anise hyssop, arnica, bergamot, betony, burdock, catmint, chamomile (Roman), chicory, chives, clary, comfrey, costmary, dandelion, dock, elecampane, feverfew, garlic, germander, ginger, goldenrod, hop, horehound, horseradish, horsetail, hyssop, lady's bedstraw, lavender (English), lemon balm, lemongrass, lovage, madder, marjoram, marsh mallow, mint, mugwort, nettle, oregano, orris, pennyroyal, red clover, saffron, sage, santolina, savory (winter), soapwort, sorrel, sweet cicely, sweet woodruff, tansy, tarragon (French), thyme (garden), valerian, violet and yarrow.

SPREADING SORREL
Common sorrel is a herbaceous perennial with a sharp, lemony flavor. Its young spring leaves are used in salads, sauces and soups. Sorrel is an aggressive grower that spreads by creeping roots. It requires a lot of hand-weeding to keep it in control.

Popular woody herbs

Woody perennials have stems that expand each year as the plants build up layers of woody growth. Some of the popular woody perennial herbs include: barberry, bay (sweet), bearberry, birch, cascara sagrada, coffee, eucalyptus, geranium (scented), lemon verbena, New Jersey tea, passionflower, rosemary, roses, sassafras and witch hazel. By learning whether a perennial herb is woody or herbaceous, you can make the most effective use of its shape and growth habits in the design of your herb garden.

HANDY HINT

At the end of the growing season, you may find perennial plants offered in garden centers at a reduced price because they have outgrown their pots. Take advantage of these if they are pest-free. If they are thickly bunched, you can slice the root ball into several sections with a knife.

FOLIAGE

One of the main reasons to grow herbs is for their flavorful or aromatic leaves. How much foliage you want to harvest will influence the size of your herb garden. You may want to grow enough basil to make a batch of pesto sauce every week. Or you may want variety for potpourris.

compound. The lacy, finely divided leaves of the carrot family, including dill, caraway and parsley, are compound leaves.

WONDROUS VARIETY

Incorporating herbs with different leaf shapes into your garden will help to give it added interest. Among the herbs you will find every shape, texture and color of leaf imaginable.

Types of leaves Leaves that are whole and undivided, like bergamot, are called simple. Leaves divided into two or more parts on the same stalk are called

Leaf shapes Leaf shapes range from the long, thin, linear leaves of lemongrass to the eye-shaped elliptical leaves of bay and the almost circular nasturtium leaf. Leaves vary in their edges as well as their shapes. A leaf with jagged edges, such as lemon balm, is

ovate · elliptical · oblong · linear · oblanceolate · obovate · lanceolate

46

toothed

entire

lobed

toothed and
lobed combination

IDENTIFYING HERBS
With experience and over time,
the kind of edge on the leaves of
your plants will help you identify
unknown herbs.

known as toothed. A leaf with smooth edges, like sweet bay, is called entire. The wavy-edged parsley leaf is referred to as lobed. Once you become familiar with herbs, you'll use these differences for identification.

Variety of color Herb leaves offer a tremendous variety of color. It's true that most leaves are green, but there are many shades of green! To vary your garden, select the blue-grays of lavender and wormwood or the brilliant green of sweet basil. Look for unusual cultivars, like deep purple basil.

Variety of texture Leaves that are striped or blotched with different colors are called variegated. Sage has several variegated cultivars, including 'Aurea,' which is yellow and green, and 'Tricolor,' which is cream, purple and green. Variegated herbs taste just as good as their green counterparts, and add color and interest to any herb garden.

Clues to herb health When shopping for herbs, the leaves can give you a good clue as to the health of the plant. Choose healthy, vigorous plants with bright, new growth. They should be free of insects and diseases. Remember to check the undersides of leaves for pests.

PLANT STEMS

The stems of your herbs not only support the
leaves, but also serve as pathways for movement
of nutrients and water between roots and leaves.
Like roots, stems are storage organs. Bulbs, such
as garlic and saffron, are actually specialized
storage stems.

Horizontal stems Some herbs
have stems, called stolons, that are
specially adapted for vegetative
reproduction. Stolons travel along
the soil surface horizontally. At
certain intervals along the stolon,
new shoots and roots will form,
giving rise to new plants. Sweet

NATURAL ARRANGEMENTS
The way the leaves are placed on the
stem is called the leaf arrangement.

palmate

trifoliate

simple

dissected

even
pinnate

odd
pinnate

woodruff and sweet violets are examples of plants that will produce stolons.

Underground stems Herbs like iris, mint and tarragon form new plants from underground stems, called rhizomes. The creeping stems of mint spread quickly, traveling just below the surface of the soil and rooting as they go. For this reason you may want to plant them in containers, preferably plastic pots or large, bottomless tubs, which you can dig into the garden bed. Otherwise you can build a wooden barrier about 14 inches (35 cm) deep around the mint patch to keep the plants under control.

PROVIDING VARIETY
Choosing herbs with different leaf arrangements will liven up the visual interest of your herb garden.

Layering Layering is a simple method of propagating herbs with stems that root easily, including tarragon, rosemary, thyme and sage. Select a long, flexible stem, then bend and lightly bury a section of it in the soil around the parent plant. You can make a small wound along the stem first, by nicking the soft wood with a knife, to encourage fast rooting. Mound soil on top of the buried stem, first holding it in place with U-shaped pins made with bent wire.

Stool layering Another method of growing new plants from stems is called stool layering. It works best with plants that have plenty of sprawling stems, like santolina, winter savory and sage. Simply mound the soil around and over the base of already established plants. Wait at least three months, then use a knife to slice away the new plants that have developed their own root systems.

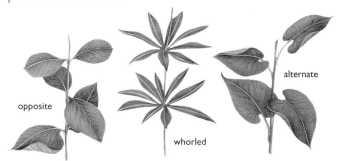

opposite

whorled

alternate

ROOT SYSTEMS

As a gardener, you probably select most plants for their aboveground appearance. But when selecting and planting herbs, you should also consider their root systems. In certain plants, like iris and ginger, the root may be the part that's used herbally.

Storage organs Roots help to hold the plant firm in the soil and provide it with a system for absorbing water and nutrients. They may also act as storage organs, as in the carrot family, holding nutrients for use in times of vigorous growth or flowering. Most herbs have a fibrous root system, made up of many fine, branching roots. Annual herbs, in particular, tend to have shallow root systems. As fibrous roots do not penetrate particularly deeply,

you'll need to pay special attention to the water requirements of such plants when rain is scarce.

Central root systems Some herbs have strong central roots, called taproots, that travel straight down in search of water and nutrients. The taproot is a single, thick, tapering organ (a carrot is actually an enlarged taproot) with thin side branch roots. In general, taprooted plants can more easily

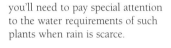

bulb

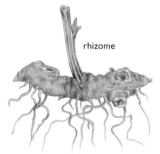

rhizome

UNDERGROUND STEMS

Although it grows in the ground, a bulb is not a root but a type of stem that's compressed and covered with scalelike leaves. A rhizome is an underground runner or stem.

COMPANION HERB
The leaves, stems and seeds of the perennial herb lovage, with its taproots, all have a savory, celery-like flavor. Some companion gardeners claim that lovage improves the growth and flavor of vegetable crops.

withstand fluctuating soil moisture conditions, but some, like parsley and lovage, are more difficult to transplant because their roots are so sensitive. They cannot survive the shock of moving.

Growing from bulbs Some herbs, like chives, saffron and garlic, grow from bulbs or similar structures. To propagate chives and saffron, lift the clumps out of the soil and divide them as you would any other plant. To propagate garlic, harvest the bulbs as usual, allowing them to dry. Save the largest bulbs with the largest cloves for replanting and use the rest in the kitchen. There's no need to clean the bulbs you plan to replant. The more they're handled and peeled, the more likely they'll rot in storage. Store them in a dark, cool location until planting time. To plant, divide the bulbs into individual cloves. Plant only the outer, large cloves, mainly because the small, inner cloves will yield smaller bulbs. Keep the small cloves in the kitchen to use soon—once separated from the bulb, they won't store well. Plant the individual cloves root-side

ROOT TIMING
When you are propagating your herbs by either of the layering methods, it's important to give the roots enough time to establish themselves so that they are less fragile. Wait three to four months, until the new plant has produced some growth and you can be sure that it has taken root. Then sever the stem connecting the old and new plants by pushing a shovel or trowel into the soil between the new plant and the old. Wait several more weeks before digging up the new plant. Plant it in a hole lined with fresh compost, or pot it in a commercially prepared potting mix for use indoors or on the patio.

down, about 1 inch (2.5 cm) deep and 6 inches (15 cm) apart in a deep bed with loosened soil. Work in plenty of organic matter, but go easy on the nitrogen. You'll find more information on propagating garlic on page 55.

HERB HARDINESS

Hardiness is the quality that enables plants to survive climactic extremes, especially cold, heat and dryness. Hardy annuals and biennials can be sown outdoors while spring or autumn frosts still threaten. Hardy perennials can be left outdoors year round even in the extreme winter cold.

Half-hardy herbs When an herb is called half-hardy, it means it requires a warm environment for successful germination but may withstand slight frosts once it's established. Calendula is a half-hardy annual that benefits from an early start indoors and can be transferred outdoors fairly early.

Tender herbs Tender annuals and perennials are those that are quickly damaged by frost or cold. Tender perennials include sweet marjoram, which must be potted and brought indoors during

cold-climate winters. Basil is a tender annual that should be started and kept indoors in spring until all danger of frost has passed.

Maintenance for hardiness
The hardiness of your herb garden is really only as good as your maintenance of the garden. Proper

MUSTARD TRAP
Mustard is a very hardy annual that is also quick to mature. As well as its culinary uses, the mustard plant makes an excellent trap crop, which means it attracts pests away from other plants.

watering is a critical part of garden maintenance. While the amount of water required varies from plant to plant, most herbs thrive in evenly moist soil. If the weather is dry, keep an eye on your herbs and water them when necessary. If the weather is wet, try removing the mulch from around the plants to let the soil dry out. It's important not to allow weeds to compete with your herbs. Weeds have adapted to grow and reproduce quickly, and will soon crowd out your herb plants.

Plant origins Knowing the origins of your herbs can help you understand why some herbs are more or less hardy than others. Many of today's popular herbs are natives of the Mediterranean region, which has a sunny climate with low humidity and moderate rainfall. Mediterranean herbs include lavender, chamomile,

BEGINNER HERBS

The following herbs are good subjects for the beginning gardener: agrimony, angelica, barberry, basil (sweet), bergamot, borage, burdock, calendula, catmint, chamomile (Roman), chicory, chives, comfrey, coriander, dandelion, dill, dock, elecampane, fennel, feverfew, geranium (scented), goldenrod, horseradish, horsetail, lady's bedstraw, lavender (English), lemon balm, lovage, marjoram, mint, mugwort, mustard, nasturtium, oregano, parsley (curled), pennyroyal (English), plantain, red clover, rosemary, rue, sage, santolina, savory (winter), soapwort, sorrel, southernwood and tansy.

thyme, borage and germander. Since they developed on poor soils, they don't demand high soil fertility and, given the right environment, they're fairly easy to grow. The origins and history of herbs can be explored further in large libraries or on the Internet.

HARDY DILL
Dill is a hardy annual plant that can be sown outdoors while spring or fall frosts still threaten. This is a very easy herb to grow, and you can use both the leaves and the seeds in cooking.

PROPAGATING HERBS

If you want to increase your herb crops, learn how to propagate them. Once you master the techniques, you'll find that your hobby will become popular among your friends as you distribute the extra plants.

SEASONAL PROPAGATING
A good time to divide your perennial herbs is from early spring through fall. The conditions are appropriate at this time because the temperature of the air is usually low and the amount of moisture in the soil is usually high. Herbs that are easily propagated by division include chives, germander, horehound, marjoram, mint, sorrel, tansy, tarragon and woodruff.

Dividing Dividing is a way to start new plants, as well as to clean up and rejuvenate the old ones. Generally, perennial herbs spread under the ground as well as above the ground. The plants usually increase in size each new growing season. If they are taking up more space than you want them to, you can divide them every few years.

The basics Start by digging around the perimeter of the plant's root system with a spade. With the last thrust, push the blade under the base of the plant and lift up the soil, roots and all. Set the clump on the ground and begin dividing it into smaller clumps by hand or with a trowel. Pry apart larger clumps or very old clumps using garden forks: Stick two garden forks back to back in the center of the clump and force it apart. Clip off or break off the young shoots from the outer side of the clump. Then cut the leaves back to within 1 inch (2.5 cm) of the roots and replant the clumps immediately, or put them in pots in a shady area until you can replant them. Plants that send out underground rhizomes, like mint, are just as easily divided without digging up the whole plant. If you follow the underground stems that sprout new plants, you can simply lift out each new plant with a spade. Reduce the large clump to several smaller plants and replant them in holes that have been lined with fresh compost.

Cuttings You can make new plants from the prunings of most perennial herbs. The best time to

54

take cuttings is in early spring or late summer through to early fall. Cut 3–5 inches (7.5–12.5 cm) of stem, just below a leaf joint (node). Remove the lower leaves. To encourage roots to form, especially on plants that are slow to root, such as bay and rosemary, dip the base of the cutting into rooting hormone. Insert the cut end of the cutting in a moist, light potting mix, making certain that several nodes have contact with the moist medium. Use small pots or any containers with good drainage. Keep the pots indoors and well away from direct sun. After six to eight weeks, check for rooting by inverting the pot onto your hand, with the cutting between your fingers. The young roots should be visible. Place your new plants in the shade for several days before planting out.

PROPAGATING GARLIC

Growing your own garlic is easy. The best time for planting is mid-fall. The bulbs will produce roots and small shoots before the ground freezes.

Save large, healthy garlic bulbs for replanting. It's best to store them in a dark, cool place.

Divide the bulbs into individual cloves. The larger outer cloves will generally yield the biggest bulbs.

Plant the cloves about 1 inch (2.5 cm) deep and 6 inches (15 cm) apart. Cover the cloves with soil rich in organic matter.

INDOOR HERBS

You can surround yourself with fresh herbs almost year round. Cuttings taken in early fall will be ready to move to the garden in spring if you nurture them indoors all winter. You can also pot up annuals and bring them indoors for winter use, or start fresh plants from seed.

PARSLEY INDOORS
Parsley is often difficult to transplant, due to its deep taproot. If you want to grow parsley for indoor use, either start seeds indoors or pot up very small self-sown plants from the garden.

Perennials You have several methods to choose from when raising a winter supply of herbs. Perennials can be grown in the garden soil in summer, and then potted up for winter indoors. At the beginning and end of the season, leave the plants in their pots in a shady spot outdoors for at least one week before moving them to their new home. This helps them adjust to the change in light from bright to moderate and vice versa. Be sure you choose a pot large enough to accommodate the root system. When digging up the plant from the garden, cut all the way around it with a spade, then gently lift the whole root ball into a pot lined with fresh potting soil. Perennials like sage, chives and rosemary also make good container plants year round—just move the pots outdoors in the summer, preferably near the water supply so you won't forget to water them.

Annuals Annual herbs for winter growing are best started fresh from seed in the fall. Sow them and care for them the same way as you start your spring seedlings indoors. Use pots that are about 3–4 inches (7.5–10 cm) deep and wide, so the plants will have enough room to grow all winter. Herbs that are difficult to transplant, like parsley, should be sown directly into deep pots and kept in their containers.

Light Your indoor herbs will need plenty of light each day for strong, vigorous growth. A sunny window is ideal, but keep the pots well away from cold windows and drafts. Once your potted herbs have filled the windows, take a step up and purchase one or more sets of fluorescent light fixtures. Use a mixture of cool white bulbs and the red or blue lights designed for plants, in order to imitate sunlight. Set the plants on shelves or plant stands so their tops are about 6–8 inches (15–20 cm) away from the lights. You can also use bricks to raise or lower individual pots as needed.

MOISTURE

Evaporation may be less indoors, or more if your house is heated in winter. Don't over-water because excess moisture encourages fungal diseases and prevents roots from getting the oxygen they need.

MAINTAINING HERB HEALTH

Like all plants, herbs show symptoms of stress from diseases, insect pests and poor conditions. Good gardeners walk through the garden at least once daily, just to be sure not to miss a distress signal. Wilting could be caused by incorrect watering or by root damage. Curled leaves could indicate insect damage, and leaves that have turned a strange color could be diseased or suffering from a nutrient deficiency. If you are familiar with your plants when they are healthy, you will notice if they are distressed.

PREVENTING PESTS

When you patrol your herb garden, watch for early signs of insect damage. The least disruptive pest-control methods, like handpicking, spraying with water or pruning, are most effective when used at the first sign of damage. Learn to identify particular pests before you use any control.

Beneficial pests Most of the insects you will discover among your herb plants won't be doing any damage at all. More likely, they're just passing through. If you're lucky, beneficial insects, like tiny parasitic wasps and beetles that have voracious appetites for harmful insects, will live among the foliage. Biological controls are nature's defense against pest attack, so if you find just a few insects around your herb garden, leave them to become food for insect predators and parasites. But keep an eye on pest population sizes so you'll see if they are getting out of hand. You'll know pests are a problem if their numbers are growing and their feeding is heavy enough to damage plants. Even small numbers of insect pests can be destructive if they carry diseases. Leafhoppers and aphids spread plant viruses; striped and spotted cucumber beetles spread bacterial wilt disease.

BAD BEETLES
Be on the lookout for adult Japanese beetles. They are metallic blue or green with coppery wing covers. Adults skeletonize leaves and eat the flowers of host plants.

Cultural controls An easy and highly effective way to correct up to 90 percent of disease and pest problems is to change the way you're growing your plants. For example, if you have put a plant that prefers full sun into a lightly shaded nook, or interplanted too tightly between taller plants, the plant can be weakened and unable to resist pest and disease attack. Be sure to keep sun-loving herbs, like basil, in sunny locations. Give well-drained soil to plants that are prone to rot. You also can avoid regular disease problems by buying species and cultivars that are disease-resistant. Double check your maintenance methods. Don't nick plants with your hoe or rake because wounds are an open invitation for pest and disease attack. Stay out of a planting when the foliage is wet so you won't spread diseases as you brush past plants. Plant companions at the proper spacing to let air circulate freely through the remaining foliage and make conditions less hospitable for fungal diseases Correct spacing also lessens the competition for water and nutrients.

Making the right diagnosis
The key to picking an effective control is knowing what pest you're dealing with. Consult a reference or general gardening book to help you correctly identify the problem. If you need outside help, contact your local botanic gardens. Some large landscaping services also have diagnostic laboratories. Once you've made the correct diagnosis, you'll need to choose a product formulated specifically for the pest on your plants. If you are growing the herbs for culinary uses, make sure to ask about an organically acceptable insecticide that will have no ill effects.

SNEAKY SNAILS
Snails are a real problem in any garden. They feed at night and can cause extensive damage to plants in just a few hours by eating large holes in the leaves.

INSECTICIDES

The aim in growing a herb garden is to use as little insecticide as possible. Once you know what pests you're dealing with, do a little research to identify the most effective and least toxic cure. Learn about the pest so you can key in on its weak areas.

Barriers and traps To stop insects before they get to your herbs, surround plants that are prone to attack by creeping pests (such as slugs and snails) with sharp or irritant products like diatomaceous earth, lime or crushed seashells. Dried hot peppers, ground up and dusted onto and around the herbs can repel root maggots. Cover plants that are routinely attacked by flying insects or their larvae with lightweight fabric supported by stakes over the top of the plants. Surround beds with copper strips to shock snails and slugs away, and protect small seedlings with cardboard tubes, about 2 inches

CONFUSING THE ENEMY
Mixed gardens of herbs, flowers, fruits and vegetables make it difficult for pests to track down their food.

(5 cm) long, that you slip over the seedlings and push halfway into the soil. With indoor plants, you can hang yellow sticky traps from stakes to draw and trap aphids.

Handpicking Occasionally you'll have to introduce more intensive methods to handle a particular pest or disease problem. You can physically pick off the pests, their egg masses or disease-spotted leaves. Crush pests or drop them into a bucket of soapy water. Put diseased leaves in the center of a hot compost pile.

Biological controls Beneficial insects are those that will prey on the destructive insects. Once you learn about the pests in your garden, you'll know which insects are their predators. You can then choose herbs that will attract the beneficial insects. Purchase enough for a single release or, for pest

DETECTIVE WORK
When there are pests on even one of your herbs, you have to proceed carefully to protect all the plants in your garden. Become a detective, finding out about beneficial insects and what companion plants can deter or trap the pests.

problems that tend to hang around, plant periodically through the growing season. In general, the most useful herbs will be the flowering herbs, such as lemon balm, thyme, cosmos, catnip, dill

and calendulas, which produce good quantities of attractive pollen and nectar.

Last resorts If the less extreme pest controls don't work, you can call on botanical insecticides and soaps. These products break down quickly after use, so they don't linger long in the environment, but they can still harm beneficial insects and animals if not used carefully. Read the label and apply the spray or dust according to the package directions. Treat only troubled plants—not the whole crop or bed—preferably in the evening, when honeybees have gone home. Try not to get spray on flowers, which may be visited by predatory wasps. Wait the full period indicated on the label before harvesting herbs for eating or storage. And always protect yourself by wearing gloves when using these products.

PREVENTING PLANT DISEASES

Plant diseases are frustrating to deal with. Symptoms like leaf wilting or yellowing, stunted growth or misshapen leaves are often the only clues you'll have when trying to diagnose the problem. They are often affected by minute organisms you can see only with a microscope.

Prevention practices Your best defense against disease organisms is prevention. When purchasing new herb plants, inspect them carefully for signs of disease and feel free to reject any that look suspicious or unhealthy. Remember that symptoms like stunted growth or off-color leaves could be due to poor growing conditions, but they could also indicate disease. Good sanitation practices are essential in the garden and greenhouse. If it is likely that you've been handling soil or plants that may be sources of infection, clean your boots and hands with a 5 percent solution of household bleach in water, or wipe them with surgical spirit. If wet weather prevails, stay away from the garden until the weather is fine again. Many disease organisms require moisture for reproduction or mobility, and they're easily spread on films of water you may carry from plant to plant. These organisms can survive even the most extreme winters in bare soil or on garden rubbish, and will flourish as soon as they are transported to a plant.

RUST SPOTS
When the leaves or stems of your herbs are affected by reddish orange spots, it is probably because of a disease called rust. The solution is to dust every two weeks with sulfur. Badly infected plants should be destroyed.

Disposing of diseased plants

Regularly inspect your plants for any signs of disease and remove unhealthy specimens. It's best to burn them, since a few pathogens that cause diseases, including bacteria, viruses, nematodes and fungi, are sufficiently hardy to survive the hottest compost piles. If burning rubbish is prohibited in your area, put the diseased plant materials in sealed bags for disposal with the household trash. Mulch your perennial herbs with regular applications of compost. Beneficial microbes in the compost suppress the development of some disease organisms.

Symptoms It's impossible to see the organisms that cause diseases in your herbs, so you have to rely on the symptoms. If the leaves are yellow-green and the plant's growth is stunted, it could be a disease known as aster yellows.

ORGANIC FUNGICIDE

Garlic is considered to have many fungicidal as well as insecticidal properties. Prepare a spray based on the recipe on page 66. It's best to use fresh garlic rather than a commercially prepared product.

You'll need to destroy the infected plants. If the leaves or stems are speckled or silvery, the problem could be thrips. Spray the plant with a soap solution. If the leaves are black and sticky or shiny, it may be sooty mold fungus. Wipe the leaves with a damp cloth. If the leaves and stems have small, hard scales, just gently scrape the bumps off the stem with a blunt knife or a fingernail. If the leaves or shoots have white spots, it could be powdery mildew. Pick off badly infected leaves and spray the rest with fungicidal soap.

65

FUNGICIDES

If your herbs are infected with disease, your control choices are fairly limited. Many gardeners have reported success using a baking soda spray against fungal diseases, like powdery mildew. For seriously infected plants, the best course is often to remove them before the disease spreads.

HOMEMADE HEALTH

Prevention is the key to managing diseases like stem rot and rust, which can cause this reddish discoloration. Use homemade fungicides on susceptible herbs before symptoms appear.

Organic fungicides Organically acceptable fungicides, such as sulfur and copper sprays, will protect your plants from disease only if they're applied before any kind of infection sets in. You can dust plants with copper or sulfur preparations if you suspect that fungal disease is a problem in your garden, but do it before or during bouts of wet weather, when plants are most likely to be infected, and before the organisms penetrate the leaf. Use low-toxic homemade fungicides on susceptible herbs before symptoms appear.

Homemade fungicides It's not difficult to make your own fungicides at home. Household baking soda can reduce the spread of some fungal diseases. Just mix together 2 teaspoons of baking soda and 8 cups of water. Use a clean spray bottle to drench your plants thoroughly with the mixture at the first sign of disease. Adding a few drops of commercial liquid dish detergent as a wetting agent will help the solution stick to leaves. You can also use garlic to control and prevent disease. Garlic is known to have fungicidal as well as insecticidal properties. Prepare an oil extract by mixing 3 ounces (85 g) of finely minced garlic into 2 teaspoons of mineral oil. Allow the mixture to stand for about 24 hours, then add 2 cups of water. Mix and strain into a glass jar for storage. When you need a fungicide, combine 2 tablespoons of the concentrate with 2 cups of water. Pour it into a garden spray that has been cleaned of any other products and spray it on the affected herbs. If necessary, add up to 1 teaspoon of liquid dish detergent to help the solution cling to foliage and stems.

Nature's nursemaids Some herbs act as nature's nursemaids, helping to heal ailing plants. Hyssop, for example, helps plants that are suffering from bacterial

Using a spray bottle for your homemade fungicides will help you to wet the plant on the underside of its leaves.

invasion. Chamomile also helps sick plants to recover. You can keep these helpful herbs in a pot and move them next to any diseased plants in your garden, or make a spray using a few drops of essential oil from these plants. Use 5 drops to every 8 cups of water in your usual gardening spray equipment. You can also use teas made from herbs in spraying equipment. Elderflower tea discourages molds on everything. Chive tea is especially useful against the gray mold that affects roses. Nettle tea combats mildew, and horsetail tea helps to protect against all kinds of fungus. Use 1 cup of fresh herbs to 2 cups of water. Boil the water, pour it onto the herbs and leave it to stand for six hours. Then strain the liquid and store. Mix 2 tablespoons of this tea into 8 cups of water in a watering can.

EFFECTIVE TREATMENT
Because it is so difficult to diagnose diseases, removing affected foliage is the best way to stop the spread of disease to newly seeded plants nearby.

67

COMPANION PLANTING

Companion planting is the technique of combining plants that will benefit each other. If your crops of vegetables are regularly attacked by insects, you can use herb companions to hide, repel or trap pests. Other herbs provide food and shelter to attract and protect beneficial insects.

SCENTED COMPANIONS
Fragrant herbs like lemon balm, scented geraniums and thyme are popular and efficient repellents of insect and animal pests. Interplant them in your flower garden.

Repelling with smells One way to use herbs in companion planting to protect your plants is to mask their odors with other powerful smells. Herbs like garlic, for instance, release deterrent aromas into the air that may chase away insects such as bean beetles and potato bugs. Mint may keep cabbage loopers off cabbage plants, and basil can discourage tomato hornworms on tomatoes. Try pungent plants as an edging around garden beds, or mix them

in among your crops of other herbs or vegetables. If you can't grow the repellent herbs close enough to your crops, you can spread clippings of the scented plants over garden beds for the same effect.

Luring pests Some herbs have an almost irresistible appeal for certain pests. Nasturtiums, for instance, are an excellent attractant plant because they're a favorite of aphids. Attractant plants can protect your crops in two ways. First, they act as decoys to lure pests away from your desirable crops. Second, they make it easier to control the pests because the insects are concentrated on a few plants. Once the pests are trapped, you can either pull the attractant plants and destroy them along with the pests or apply some other type of control measure to the infested plants.

Sheltering beneficial insects
Not all insects are garden enemies. Many actually help your garden grow by eating plant pests. You can encourage these beneficial creatures to make a home in your garden by planting their favorite flowering plants. Growing dill, for example, can attract pest-eating spiders, lacewings and parasitic wasps, which will help to control caterpillars on cabbages, beetles on cucumbers and aphids on lettuces.

Complementary crops Some herbs make ideal vegetable garden companions because they don't compete, even when planted close together in small spaces. Deep-rooted plants occupy different soil zones to shallow-rooted plants, so their roots can draw on different nutrient sources. Crops that need lots of nutrients combine well with light feeders.

MIXED PLANTINGS
Mixing flowering and fruiting crops can give you a garden that's attractive as well as productive. In addition, beneficial insects are attracted to mixed plantings because they can find plenty of food and shelter.

HOSTILE HERBS

Just as some plants grow especially well together, a few are able to keep other plants from crowding in around them. This is called allelopathy. Allelopathic plants release inhibitory chemicals into the soil or air—a neat trick for making sure nothing competes for rooting space and moisture.

Chemical release Chemical compounds released by some living plants and decomposing plants—including legumes, grains, brassicas and marigolds—can lower the yields of existing crop plants, kill seedlings and limit seed germination. The herb gray sage, for instance, releases a volatile compound that drifts to the earth nearby and stops the seedling growth of many species. Common wormwood can interfere with plant growth, especially when interplanted with other herbs,

WORRYING WORMWOOD

Companion gardeners note that few plants thrive when planted near wormwood. Glandular hairs on the surface of the leaves produce volatile oils and the inhibiting toxin absinthin. Rain or watering washes the substances from leaves, and poisons nearby plants.

and fennel is known to inhibit the growth of all plants. Parsley is a poor companion for lettuce, and growing any kind of bean near garlic will produce a poor result, no matter what the soil and weather conditions.

Dealing with difficult plants
In many cases, it's hard to identify when allelopathy is at work. The actual effect can be influenced by the soil, the amount of rainfall and the plants themselves. If some of your crops are growing poorly and you've ruled out diseases and nutrient imbalances, consider that allelopathy might be the cause and try growing those plants elsewhere next year.

When companion planting doesn't work
It's a good idea to experiment with companion planting and keep a record of your efforts. Even failures can be useful for future reference. For example, you may find that a combination that was highly recommended by someone else simply doesn't work in your garden. If this happens, try to figure out why the combination didn't work: Was it due to that early heat spell that caused pests to emerge sooner than expected? Or perhaps you forgot to pull out the trap crop before pests spread to your good plants? If your soil is rich in nutrients, for example, the pungency of your herbs tends to be weakened and they may be less effective as pest repellents. If a combination performs poorly the first year, don't give up immediately; consider giving it at least one more try. Use your notes to compare the results for both years and put the information to work for your garden.

ERSTWHILE COMPANION
Dill is a useful plant in the companion garden, thanks to its big, airy umbels of many tiny flowers, which attract beneficial insects. However, many growers believe that dill is an enemy of carrots and tomatoes.

HARVESTING
AND
STORING HERBS

One of the first rules to learn about growing herbs is to harvest them early in the morning. The best picking time is just after the morning dew has dried, but before the Sun has had a chance to warm them. The reason is that essential oils—those mysterious components that give herbs their flavor and fragrance—deteriorate when exposed to heat. There's nothing wrong with morning dew, but wet leaves require a longer drying period before you can store them. For the same reason, refrain from harvesting on rainy days. A cool, dry, sunny morning is best.

HARVESTING FOR THE KITCHEN

The intended use of your herbs, the maturity of the plant and the climate all influence the time of harvesting. You need not be so fussy if you plan to use fresh herbs immediately. Just pick and use these whenever you need them.

RARE HARVEST
Saffron threads are harvested for their rich flavor. The difficulty of collecting the threads is the reason saffron is so expensive to purchase.

Optimum flavor For the best flavor, harvest herbs just before the buds open, which is when the concentration of essential oils is greatest. It's especially important to follow this rule if you're harvesting a large quantity of herbs to dry or freeze for winter or if you're making a bouquet garni to flavor stocks and sauces. For garnish or flavor, harvest fresh blossoms like chives, borage or calendula at full bloom or just before. If you're picking chamomile flowers to use in making tea, pinch them off when they are fully open.

Growing for seeds Herbs grown for their seeds should be harvested after the seeds have turned from green to brown—but make sure you harvest them before they begin to fall from the plant. If you're growing biennial plants, like caraway, for their seeds, avoid harvesting the foliage the first year. The more energy the plants can make and store, the more seeds they can set the following year.

Root herbs Harvest herbs grown for their roots when the roots are fully developed in the fall. Carefully scrape the soil away from the base of the plant and use a sharp knife to harvest some of the largest roots. Or you could use a spading fork to lift the whole plant out of the ground for an easier harvest. Either way, make sure that you leave some roots so the plant can re-establish itself and provide you with future harvests. Replant or backfill with the soil you removed and water the plant to settle it back into the soil. Scrub the harvested roots well before using or drying.

How to harvest Use sharp scissors or a garden knife when harvesting your herbs. If you're collecting leaves, cut the whole stem before stripping away the foliage. With small-leaved perennials, like rosemary and thyme, save only the leaves and discard the stems—or use them for potpourris. When harvesting herbs that spread from a central growing point, like parsley and

sorrel, harvest the outer stems or leaves first. If you're collecting leaves or flowers from bushy plants, do so from the top of the plant; new growth will come from below. Of course, you can

harvest foliage and flowers from both perennials and annuals continuously if you're just snipping a few leaves and blooms here and there to collect the ingredients for a recipe.

HANDY HERBS
Bay, thyme, parsley, chives, mint and sage are all useful herbs in the kitchen and can be used fresh from the herb garden or planter pot, or dried.

HARVESTING FOR CRAFTS

To dry your herbs for use in crafts, bunching them as you collect them saves handling time later. Collect enough stems to make a bundle and wrap a rubber band over the cut ends. When harvesting annuals in fall, pull and hang the whole plant, cutting away the roots and soil.

Harvesting when flowering

Most of the fragrant herbs that are used as wreath backing or as the base of dried arrangements should be cut when they're flowering. If you're collecting flowers such as yarrow for dried arrangements, wait until they are in full bloom or just before. Cut them with plenty of stem. Southernwood may be cut back by a third after its first flush of spring growth, then again in late summer. Collect rose petals at full bloom, after the morning dew has dried. When cutting lavender, harvest the whole stem with the attached flower heads, just before the blooms are fully opened

LAVENDER FOR CRAFT

Lavender flowers that are harvested just before the blooms open will keep their fragrance after drying.

Drying in bunches Herbs with long stems, like lavender, mint and yarrow, are easy to dry in bunches. Select only the highest quality foliage and blossoms, removing any dead or wilted leaves. Make bunches about 1 inch (2.5 cm) in diameter for quick drying. You can tie the bunches with string, leaving a loop for hanging, but small rubber bands are easier to use.

Washing herbs Herbs retain their best qualities if they're left unwashed until it's time to use them. Some growers recommend sprinkling the plants the day before harvesting, to wash away the dust. If your plants are surrounded by a mulch that protects them from contact with soil, you may not have to wash them. If they are gritty with soil, however, you can swish them through cold water and hang them in shade to drip.

Taking care of dust Dust can cling to the moisture of freshly harvested plants, so try the brown paper bag technique. When you harvest the herbs, put the bunches inside paper bags. Punch a hole in the base of the bag, pull the stems through and fasten them together. Hang the bag in a cool, dry place. To increase air circulation, cut flaps in the side of the bag. After a week, check a few bags to make sure the herbs are drying and free of mold. They may take two weeks to become crumbly. When they're dry, remove the stems and spread the leaves on a baking sheet. Bake in an oven, set at about 100°F (38°C), for several minutes to complete the drying process.

BAGGING THE DUST
The paper bag technique of harvesting herbs makes certain that they will dry free of dust. Dust can affect the color and aroma of your dried herbs.

77

DRYING HERBS

Some growers claim that dried, summer-grown herbs have a better flavor than herbs grown indoors in winter. If you enjoy cooking with herbs, you may want to try preserving some of your summer garden's bounty for use in winter recipes. Most herbs dry easily.

Where to dry herbs It's best to dry herbs in a place that is dark with good ventilation. Depending on what the weather is like, you may find it necessary to speed up the process with dehumidifiers, fans or an air conditioner. The most suitable weather conditions for air drying are low humidity and soft breezes. Drying screens and bunches can be placed in a dry attic, around the hot-water heater, on top of the refrigerator or in a gas oven with a pilot light. Barns make excellent drying sheds as long as they are shady and well ventilated. In summer, some gardeners dry their herbs on small screens placed inside the car. Just cover the herbs with a single layer of paper toweling and park the car in light shade. If the weather hasn't cooperated and the drying process seems painfully slow, you can speed up the action in your oven. Place your herbs on baking sheets and turn the oven temperature to its lowest setting. Monitor progress until leaves are crispy dry. You'll find more information on the different methods of oven-drying on page 80.

PRETTY PETALS
The petals of your herb plants and other flowering plants can be harvested and dried in the same way as the foliage of the plants.

Hanging the bunches Fasten your bunches of herbs on wire clothes hangers. Holding the bunched stems along one side of the horizontal wire of the hanger, pull a loop of the rubber band down and then up over the wire. Pull the band over the stems and release it. Hanging a full hanger in one spot is easier than having separate bunches all over the place. Have a separate hanger for each herb species or cultivar to make organization easy. You can label each bunch or each hanger. When you're ready to use the herbs, simply pull the bunch down to release it.

PRETTY BUNCHES
Dried herbs store best in cool, dark places. If you like the look of the bunches, it's fine to hang some around your home for decoration. But store herbs that you plan to use for cooking in airtight jars.

DRYING HERBS continued

Drying on screens Herbs with short stems and small leaves, like thyme, are difficult to bunch. The best drying method is simply to snip off the foliage with scissors and spread it on a screen in a single layer. You can also dry herbs with large leaves on screens, but first strip the foliage from the stems. Hold the stems upside down in one hand while running the other hand down the stem. Loose herb blossoms and flower petals can be dried on screens. Remember to stir the herbs once a day on the screens for even drying. If the herbs are fine, spread a paper towel or sheet of paper on the screen first. Your herbs should be dry in seven to ten days.

PLENTIFUL HERBS
It may be worth investing in a food dehydrator so you can quickly dry fast-growing herbs like oregano. Use the oven-drying method.

Drying in the oven
Probably the best method for drying herbs is oven-drying, since the herbs dry quickly and retain their aromatic oils. In a conventional oven, spread the herbs one layer deep on paper toweling that has been set on baking sheets. It's best to start with the temperature set at around 100°F (38°C). If you can smell the herbs immediately, lower the heat to avoid losing essential oils. Stir once every half hour. Drying should be complete in three to six hours. Herbs with fleshy leaves will take longer to dry than those with tiny or thin leaves, so it's wise not to mix different leaf types in one batch. Remove the herbs when they are crispy dry, and before they turn brown.

Drying in the microwave You can also dry herbs in a microwave oven. Sandwich the herbs between sheets of microwave-safe paper towels. Put a cup of water in the microwave while drying the herbs. Leave the herbs in the oven for about one minute on a low setting, then Remove them and check for dryness. If they're still a little bit moist, repeat the process for a few seconds. Watch the herbs carefully during drying, and stop the process if any sparks appear. If your herbs turn brown or black, try heating for shorter periods.

Drying herb seeds Many of the herbs you'll grow are used for their seeds. If you're collecting caraway, coriander, dill or other herb seeds for the kitchen, snip off the seed heads when they've turned brown. You'll have to blanch them in order to destroy the seemingly invisible insect pests that can hide inside. Gather the seeds in a piece of muslin and dip them in boiling water, or place the seeds in a sieve and pour boiling water over them. Spread them on paper or a mesh screen to dry in the sun. Once they are dry, store them in an airtight container. If you plan to sow the seeds you've saved, skip the blanching. Dry them in the sun before transferring them to a cool, dry location.

LOOKING AFTER YOUR CROP

If your herbs are grown, harvested and dried properly, they will remain green and fragrant for a long time. Scentless brown herbs will have little flavor.

Oven-drying reduces the time it takes for your herbs to dry and ensures the herbs won't rot.

If you intend to store your herbs whole, make sure they are completely dry before you store them.

You can construct your own screens with scrap lumber and window screening, then set them on bricks so that air circulates.

STORING HERBS

You've put a great deal of effort into growing, harvesting and drying your herbs. The last important step is to carefully store them. Store dried herb foliage, blossoms, roots or seeds in airtight containers away from bright light. Or you may want to freeze your herbs instead.

Airtight containers Your herbs will store best in glass jars with suction lids or in canning jars with rubber seals. You can also pack the dried materials into resealable plastic bags, squeezing out the air before you seal them. When your herbs have dried thoroughly, strip the leaves from their stems or remove them from the drying screens. Discard stems or save them to add to potpourris. If you're saving herbs for culinary use, crush them or push them through a coarse strainer. Leaves and blossoms saved for tea can be left whole. Crumble dried roots to sizes that will fit their use. Label your containers, since all dried herbs tend to look the same. It's fine to dry your herbs on top of the refrigerator, but don't store them there. Ideally, dried herbs should be kept cool and dry. If you like the look of herb bunches and arrangements hanging about the kitchen, make them especially

SUITABLE STORAGE
Remember to choose a container that will suit the use of your herb foliage. Once your herbs have been dried, strip the leaves from the stems. If the leaves are to be stored crushed, the opening of the container need not be as wide as if they are to be left whole.

decorative with added ribbons or lace and attractive jars and use them as ornaments, but keep culinary herbs in clean, dry airtight containers.

Freezing herbs If you have more freezer space than cupboard space, you may want to freeze your herbs. Chervil, dill, fennel, marjoram, mint, parsley and tarragon freeze very well. Herb growers report mixed results with coriander and chives—it seems they freeze very well or very poorly! You'll have to experiment, and keep records of what works best for you. Harvest the herbs at their peak and wash them gently but thoroughly, then pat dry. You can chop the herbs by hand or in the food processor until the pieces are the right size to add to soups or other recipes. Pack them in freezer bags, squeezing out the air until you have a flat layer of herbs,

and seal. Be sure to label the bags, since most frozen herbs look alike in the middle of winter. When you're ready to use them, simply break off a corner or as much as you need and return the bag to the freezer. Some herb savers purée fresh herbs with water or oil. They pour the purée into ice-cube trays and, when the cubes are solid, move them to labeled freezer bags. Herb cubes are easy to use—just toss them into soups or stews. Frozen basil retains the best quality when puréed in olive oil. It's easy to prepare winter pesto— mix in the cheese, pine nuts and garlic as the basil thaws.

ALTERNATIVE FREEZING
With some herbs, like lovage and thyme, you may have more success if you blanch the herbs first. Holding the stems, dip the herbs in boiling water. When the color brightens, they are ready. It takes only a few seconds.

After blanching, place the herbs on clean paper towels by the bunch to cool.

When air-cooled and dry, lay the herbs out in single layers on wax paper, then roll up and label.

Store in the freezer for enjoyment all winter long. Break off as much as you want and use frozen.

PART TWO

PLANT BY
PLANT GUIDE

PLANT BY PLANT GUIDE

This quick gardening guide is a starting point; it will
help you decide what to plant. The coldest hardiness
zone for perennials is shown in brackets (see page 310).

HERB	GROWTH FORM AND SIZE	PREFERRED CLIMATE	PRIMARY USES
Agrimony *Agrimonia eupatoria*	Perennial 2–5 feet (0.6–1.5 m)	Cool (Zone 6)	Medicinal herb (dried foliage)
Aloe *Aloe vera*	Succulent evergreen perennial 1 foot (30 cm)	Warm (Zone 10); grow indoors in cooler Zones	Medicinal herb, cosmetic preparation (peeled leaf or extracted mucilage)
Angelica *Angelica archangelica*	Perennial 5–8 feet (1.5–2.4 m)	Cool (Zone 4)	Medicinal herb, confection, liqueur flavoring (dried roots or foliage)
Anise *Pimpinella anisum*	Annual 2 feet (60 cm)	Cool	Medicinal and flavoring herb (dried seeds, fresh leaves)
Anise hyssop *Agastache foeniculum*	Perennial 3 feet (90 cm)	Cool (Zone 5)	Herbal tea (fresh or dried foliage, dried flowers)
Arnica *Arnica montana*	Perennial 2 feet (60 cm)	Cool (Zone 6)	Medicinal herb for external use (dried flowers, roots)
Barberry *Berberis vulgaris*	Deciduous shrub 6–8 feet (1.8–2.4 m)	Cool (Zone 4)	Medicinal herb, dyeing (berries, dried bark, dried root)
Basil, sweet *Ocimum basilicum*	Annual 1–2 feet (30–60 cm)	Mild	Culinary herb (fresh or dried foliage)
Bay, sweet *Laurus nobilis*	Evergreen shrub or tree 6–12 feet (1.8–3.6 m)	Mild (Zone 8)	Culinary herb (dried leaves)
Bearberry *Arctostaphylos uva-ursi*	Creeping evergreen shrub to 3 inches (7.5 cm)	Cool (Zone 2)	Medicinal herb (dried leaves)

HERB	GROWTH FORM AND SIZE	PREFERRED CLIMATE	PRIMARY USES
Bergamot *Monarda didyma*	Perennial 3–4 feet (90–120 cm)	Cool (Zone 4)	Herbal tea, crafts, salad herb (dried leaves, fresh or dried flowers)
Betony *Stachys officinalis*	Perennial 3 feet (90 cm)	Cool (Zone 4)	Medicinal herb, dyeing (dried leaves)
Birch *Betula spp.*	Deciduous trees 40–90 feet (12–27 m)	Cool (Zone 4)	Beverages (dried leaves and bark)
Borage *Borago officinalis*	Annual 2–3 feet (60–90 cm)	Cool	Culinary herb, flavoring drinks (fresh or pickled leaves, candied flowers)
Burdock *Arctium lappa*	Biennial 3–10 feet (1–3 m)	Cool (Zone 3)	Medicinal herb, vegetable (fresh or dried roots)
Calendula *Calendula officinalis*	Annual 1–2 feet (30–60 cm)	Mild or cool	Medicinal and culinary herb (fresh, dried or preserved flowers)
Caraway *Carum carvi*	Biennial 1–2 feet (30–60 cm)	Cool (Zone 3)	Culinary, medicinal, and flavoring herb (dried seeds, fresh young leaves)
Cascara sagrada *Rhamnus purshiana*	Deciduous shrub 5–25 feet (1.5–7.5 m)	Mild (Zone 7)	Medicinal herb (dried bark)
Catmint *Nepeta cataria*	Perennial 1–3 feet (30–90 cm)	Cool (Zone 4)	Culinary and medicinal herb, cat attractant (fresh or dried foliage)
Cayenne pepper *Capsicum annuum*	Annual or tender perennial 1–2 feet (30–60 cm)	Warm	Culinary herb (fresh or dried fruits)
Chamomile, Roman *Chamaemelum nobile*	Creeping perennial 6–9 inches (15–23 cm)	Cool (Zone 3)	Medicinal herb (dried flowers)
Chervil *Anthriscus cerefolium*	Annual 1–2 feet (30–60 cm)	Cool	Culinary herb (fresh or dried leaves)

PLANT BY PLANT GUIDE continued

HERB	GROWTH FORM AND SIZE	PREFERRED CLIMATE	PRIMARY USES
Chicory *Cichorium intybus*	Perennial 3–5 feet (0.9–1.5 m)	Cool (Zone 3)	Culinary herb, vegetable, beverage (fresh leaves, dried roots)
Chives *Allium schoenoprasum*	Perennial 6–12 inches (15–30 cm)	Cool (Zone 3)	Culinary herb (fresh or dried leaves)
Clary *Salvia sclarea*	Perennial 2–5 feet (0.6–1.5 m)	Cool (Zone 4)	Culinary herb, potpourri (fresh or dried leaves)
Coffee *Coffea arabica*	Evergreen shrub or small tree 15–40 feet (4.5–12 m)	Warm (Zone 10); grow indoors in cooler Zones	Beverage (dried and roasted seeds)
Comfrey *Symphytum officinale*	Perennial 3–5 feet (0.9–1.5 m)	Cool (Zone 3)	Medicinal herb for external use (fresh or dried leaves, dried root)
Coriander *Coriandrum sativum*	Annual 1–3 feet (30–90 cm)	Mild	Culinary herb, potpourri (fresh or dried leaves, seeds)
Costmary *Chrysanthemum balsamita*	Perennial 1–3 feet (30–90 cm)	Cool (Zone 4)	Culinary herb, potpourri (fresh or dried leaves)
Dandelion *Taraxacum officinale*	Perennial 6–12 inches (15–30 cm)	Cool (Zone 2)	Culinary and medicinal herb, beverages (fresh leaves, dried roots)
Dill *Anethum graveolens*	Annual 3 feet (90 cm)	Cool	Culinary herb (fresh and dried leaves, dried seeds)
Dock *Rumex spp.*	Perennial 1–4 feet (30–120 cm)	Cool (Zone 5)	Medicinal herb (dried roots)
Elecampane *Inula helenium*	Perennial 4–6 feet (1.2–1.8 m)	Cool (Zone 4)	Culinary and medicinal herb (dried roots)
Eucalypts *Eucalyptus spp.*	Evergreen trees 5–300 feet (1.5–95 m)	Mild (Zone 8)	Medicinal herb (oil distilled from leaves), crafts

HERB	GROWTH FORM AND SIZE	PREFERRED CLIMATE	PRIMARY USES
Fennel *Foeniculum vulgare*	Perennial (grown as annual) 4 feet (1.2 m)	Mild (Zone 6)	Culinary herb (young leaves, bulbous leaf bases, seeds)
Fenugreek *Trigonella foenum-graecum*	Annual 1–2 feet (30–60 cm)	Mild	Culinary and medicinal herb (dried seeds)
Feverfew *Tanacetum parthenium*	Perennial 2–3 feet (60–90 cm)	Mild (Zone 5)	Crafts (dried flowers)
Garlic *Allium sativum*	Bulbous perennial to 2 feet (60 cm)	Cool (Zone 5)	Culinary herb (bulbs)
Geranium, scented *Pelargonium spp..*	Evergreen shrub to 3 feet (90 cm)	Mild (Zone 10); annual in cooler Zones	Potpourri, culinary herb (dried or fresh leaves)
Germander *Teucrium chamaedrys*	Shrubby perennial to 2 feet (60 cm)	Mild (Zone 5)	Medicinal herb, ornamental (dried flowers and foliage)
Ginger *Zingiber officinale*	Perennial 2–4 feet (60–120 cm)	Warm (Zone 9)	Culinary herb (fresh or dried root)
Goldenrod *Solidago spp.*	Perennial 3–7 feet (0.9–2.1 m)	Cool (Zone 4)	Medicinal herb, crafts (dried leaves and flowers)
Hop *Humulus lupulus*	Climbing perennial 20–30 feet (6–9 m)	Cool (Zone 3)	Medicinal herb, flavoring of beverages (dried female flowers)
Horehound *Marrubium vulgare*	Perennial 2–3 feet (60–90 cm)	Mild (Zone 4)	Medicinal herb, flavoring of beverages and candies (dried leaves)
Horsereadish *Armoracia rusticana*	Perennial 2–3 feet (60–90 cm)	Cool (Zone 5)	Culinary herb
Horsetail *Equisetum spp.*	Perennial 4–18 inches (10–45 cm)	Cool (Zone 2)	Ornamental, scouring of utensils (fresh or dried stems)

HERB	GROWTH FORM AND SIZE	PREFERRED CLIMATE	PRIMARY USES
Hyssop *Hyssopus officinalis*	Shrubby perennial 1–2 feet (30–60 cm)	Cool (Zone 3)	Medicinal and culinary herb (fresh or dried leaves)
Lady's bedstraw *Galium verum*	Perennial to 3 feet (90cm)	Cool (Zone 3)	Ornamental, medicinal herb (dried flowering plant)
Lavender, English *Lavandula angustifolia*	Shrubby perennial 2–3 feet (60 –90 cm)	Mild (Zone 5)	Crafts, potpourri (distilled oil, dried flowers)
Lemon balm *Melissa officinalis*	Perennial 1–2 feet (30–60 cm)	Cool (Zone 4)	Culinary herb, herbal teas (fresh or dried leaves)
Lemongrass *Cymbopogon citratus*	Perennial to 6 feet (1.8 m)	Warm (Zone 10)	Culinary herb, potpourri, herbal tea (fresh inner leaves, distilled oil)
Lemon verbena *Aloysia triphylla*	Evergreen shrub 5–10 feet (1.5–3 m)	Mild (Zone 9)	Culinary herb, potpourri (fresh or dried leaves)
Lovage *Levisticum officinale*	Perennial to 6 feet (1.8 m)	Cool (Zone 5)	Culinary herb, vegetable (fresh young leaves and stalks, dried leaves and seeds)
Madagascar periwinkle *Catharanthus roseus*	Annual or short-lived perennial to 2 feet (60 cm)	Warm (Zone 9)	Ornamental
Madder *Rubia tinctorum*	Trailing perennial to 4 feet (1.2 m)	Mild (Zone 7)	Medicinal herb, dyeing (fresh or dried root)
Marjoram *Origanum majorana*	Perennial to 2 feet (60 cm)	Mild (Zone 9)	Culinary herb (fresh or dried leaves)
Marsh mallow *Althaea officinalis*	Perennial 4–5 feet (1.2–1.5 m)	Cool (Zone 3)	Medicinal herb, vegetable (fresh leaves, dried flowers, fresh or dried roots)
Mint *Mentha spp.*	Perennial to 30 inches (75 cm)	Mild (Zone 5)	Flavoring of beverages, confections, potpourri (fresh or dried leaves)

HERB	GROWTH FORM AND SIZE	PREFERRED CLIMATE	PRIMARY USES
Mugwort *Artemisia vulgaris*	Perennial 3–6 feet (90–180 cm)	Cool (Zone 4)	Crafts, insect repellent (dried leaves)
Mustard *Brassica spp.*	Annual 4–6 feet (1.2–1.8 m)	Cool	Culinary herb (dried seeds, seed oil)
Nasturtium *Tropaeolum majus*	Annual 1–2 feet (30–60 cm)	Cool	Culinary herb (fresh leaves and flowers, pickled buds)
Nettle *Urtica dioica*	Perennial 2–6 feet (60–180 cm)	Cool (Zone 5)	Medicinal herb, vegetable, fiber (fresh or dried foliage)
New Jersey tea *Ceanothus americanus*	Deciduous shrub 2–3 feet (60–90 cm)	Cool (Zone 4)	Medicinal herb, herbal tea (fresh or dried leaves)
Oregano *Origanum vulgare*	Perennial 12–30 inches (30–75 cm)	Mild (Zone 5)	Culinary herb (fresh or dried foliage)
Orris *Iris x germanica*	Perennial to 30 inches (75 cm)	Mild (Zone 5)	Potpourri (dried rhizome)
Parsley, curled *Petroselinum crispum*	Biennial 8–12 inches (20–30 cm)	Mild (Zone 5)	Culinary herb (fresh or dried leaves)
Passionflower *Passiflora incarnata*	Climber (semi-woody) 25–30 feet (7.5–9 m)	Mild (Zone 7)	Edible fruit
Pennyroyal, English *Mentha pulegium*	Perennial to 1 foot (30 cm)	Mild (Zone 5)	Insect repellent, perfumery (fresh or dried shoots in bud, distilled oil)
Pipsissewa *Chimaphila umbellata*	Evergreen perennial to 10 inches (25 cm)	Cool (Zone 4)	Medicinal and culinary herb (fresh or dried leaves)
Plantain *Plantago major*	Perennial 6–18 inches (15–45 cm)	Cool (Zone 2)	Medicinal herb, dyeing (fresh or dried leaves, dried roots)

HERB	GROWTH FORM AND SIZE	PREFERRED CLIMATE	PRIMARY USES
Red clover *Trifolium pratense*	Perennial 1–2 feet (30–60 cm)	Cool (Zone 5)	Medicinal herb, herbal tea (fresh or dried flowerheads)
Rosemary *Rosmarinus officinalis*	Evergreen shrub 2–6 feet (60–180 cm)	Mild (Zone 8)	Culinary and medicinal herb, potpourri (fresh or dried leaves, distilled oil)
Roses *Rosa spp.*	Deciduous shrubs or woody climbers 2–30 feet (0.6–9 m)	Cool (Zone 4)	Medicinal herb, herbal tea, perfumery (dried flower petals, fresh or dried fruit)
Rue *Ruta graveolens*	Perennial 2–3 feet (60–90 cm)	Mild (Zone 4)	Ornamental, crafts (fresh or dried leaves and flowers)
Safflower *Carthamus tinctorius*	Annual 2–3 feet (60–90 cm)	Cool	Dyeing, vegetable oil (dried flowers, seeds)
Saffron *Crocus sativus*	Bulbous perennial to 12 inches (30 cm)	Cool (Zone 6)	Spice, dyeing (dried stigmas)
Sage *Salvia officinalis*	Perennial or subshrub 1–2 feet (30–60 cm)	Mild (Zone 4)	Culinary and medicinal herb (fresh or dried leaves)
Santolina *Santolina chamaecyparissus*	Perennial or subshrub to 2 feet (60 cm)	Mild (Zone 6)	Insect repellent, perfumery, crafts (dried foliage and flowerheads)
Sassafras *Sassafras albidum*	Deciduous tree 20–60 feet (6–18 m)	Cool (Zone 5)	Ornamental, perfumery (dried root, distilled oil)
Savory, winter *Satureja montana*	Perennial or subshrub 6–12 inches (15–30 cm)	Cool (Zone 6)	Culinary herb (fresh or dried leaves)
Soapwort *Saponaria officinalis*	Perennial 1–2 feet (30–60 cm)	Cool (Zone 3)	Soap substitute, medicinal herb (fresh leaves, fresh or dried roots)
Sorrel *Rumex spp.*	Perennial 30–36 inches (75–90 cm)	Cool (Zone 5)	Culinary herb, salad vegetable (fresh leaves)

HERB	GROWTH FORM AND SIZE	PREFERRED CLIMATE	PRIMARY USES
Southernwood *Artemisia abrotanum*	Perennial 3–6 feet (0.9–1.8 m)	Mild (Zone 4)	Crafts, insect repellent, potpourri (dried foliage)
Sweet cicely *Myrrhis odorata*	Perennial to 3 feet (90 cm)	Cool (Zone 3)	Culinary herb (fresh or dried leaves, dried seeds, dried roots)
Sweet woodruff *Galium odoratum*	Perennial 8–12 inches (20–30 cm)	Cool (Zone 3)	Crafts, potpourri, insect repellent (dried foliage)
Tansy *Tanacetum vulgare*	Perennial 3–4 feet (90–120 cm)	Cool (Zone 4)	Insect repellent, crafts, dyeing (fresh or dried flowering branches)
Tarragon, French *Artemisia dracunculus*	Perennial to 2 feet (60 cm)	Cool (Zone 4)	Culinary herb (fresh or dried foliage)
Thyme, garden *Thymus vulgaris*	Perennial or subshrub 6–15 inches (15–38 cm)	Mild (Zone 5)	Culinary and medicinal herb (fresh or dried foliage)
Valerian *Valeriana officinalis*	Perennial 3–5 feet (0.9–1.5 m)	Cool (Zone 4)	Ornamental, medicinal herb (dried roots)
Vervain, European *Verbena officinalis*	Perennial (grown as annual) 1–3 feet (30–90 cm)	Cool (Zone 5)	Ornamental
Violet *Viola odorata*	Perennial 4–6 inches (10–15 cm)	Mild (Zone 5)	Confectionery, perfumery (dried flowers, leaves, roots, candied flowers)
Witch hazel *Hamamelis virginiana*	Deciduous shrub 8–15 feet (2.4–4.5 m)	Mild (Zone 4)	Medicinal herb (bark, leaves, flowering twigs)
Wormwood *Artemisia absinthium*	Perennial to 4 feet (1.2 m)	Cool (Zone 4)	Crafts, insect repellent (dried foliage and flowers)
Yarrow *Achillea millefolium*	Perennial to 3 feet (90 cm)	Cool (Zone 2)	Crafts, dyeing (dried flowers)

ALOE

Aloe barbadensis [A. vera] Liliaceae

For color and textural contrast, grow several of the more than 300 perennial species of succulent aloe. The long, tapering leaves are ornamented with soft spines and contain a gel that is medicinal as well as cosmetic.

Aloe gel is sold commercially.

Best climate and site Zones 9–10, or greenhouse not below 41°F (5°C). Prefers full sun but tolerates light shade.

Ideal soil conditions Well-drained soil low in organic matter.

Growing guidelines Separate new shoots from established plants. In cool climates, plant in pots and move them indoors in winter. Aloes thrive with little attention. Indoors, avoid overwatering and mix coarse sand with the potting soil to facilitate good drainage.

Growing habit Variable height; stemless rosette of spiny, tapered, succulent leaves.

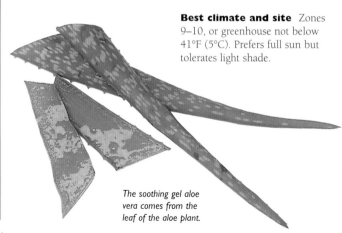

The soothing gel aloe vera comes from the leaf of the aloe plant.

Flowering time Rarely flowers in cool climates; drooping, tubular, yellow flowers atop a stalk that can grow up to 3 feet (90cm) tall.

Pest and disease prevention Spray with insecticidal soap to control mealybugs, or purchase biological controls. Make sure it is pest-free before bringing indoors.

Harvesting and storing Cut leaves for gel as needed; remove outer leaves first.

Special tips Grow on sunny windowsills in the kitchen and bathroom.

Precautions Unsafe to use internally.

EASY ALOE
The aloe plant is a succulent that thrives with little attention.

ANGELICA, EUROPEAN

Angelica archangelica Umbelliferae

This tall, sweet-scented herb resembles its close relatives, parsley and coriander. Leaf stems can be candied and used as cake decorations, or the seeds and the dried root can be infused and taken as a tea. The seeds are also used to flavor drinks, especially gin.

Best climate and site Zones 6–9. Full sun or partial shade.

Ideal soil conditions Damp garden soil.

Growing guidelines Can only be increased from seed, which germinates poorly if sown too deeply. When sowing, just press into the soil surface and barely cover. Best sown in situ in late spring. Seedlings do not transplant well, so ideally sow three to four seeds in a cluster at stations about 3 feet (90 cm) apart and thin to the strongest seedling. Alternatively, sow two or three seeds together in 4 inch (10 cm) containers of potting soil and place in a cold frame or greenhouse.

ATTRACTIVE ANGELICA
Angelica forms a striking clump of broad, lobed leaves. Its scented flowers attract beneficial insects.

seedling and set outside when each plant has three or four true leaves. If sowing is made in a heated greenhouse in early spring, an earlier crop can be expected. Angelica can be grown to maturity in a container. Ideally plant it in a 10-inch (25-cm) pot filled with rich compost and either sow direct or set one young plant in the middle. Water regularly and apply a liquid manure at 10–14 day intervals as soon as roots show at the drainage hole.

Angelica is used in herbal ointments for ailing eyes.

Growing habit Hardy biennial; height 5–8 feet (1.5–2.4 m); stout, hollow stems with broad, lobed leaves.

Flowering time Blooms the second or third year in June or July, then dies. Deadheading will prolong the life of the plant.

Pest and disease prevention
Wash aphids from seed heads with a spray of water. Be wary also of crown rot.

Harvesting and storing
Collect small stalks the first summer. Pick stems and leaves in spring of the second year; harvest the ripe seeds before they fall, dry them and store them in airtight containers in the refrigerator.

Special tips In potpourris, seeds act as a fixative.

PROVIDING SHADE
Angelica's tall stems will shade out plants growing beneath it. It can be used to provide effective shade for summer lettuces.

Precautions Some scientists say that angelica is a suspected carcinogen, while others say it contains an anticancer compound. Research is continuing.

ANISE

Pimpinella anisum Umbelliferae

Use these licorice-scented leaves and seeds in salads, especially when combined with apples. The crushed, aromatic seeds enhance the fragrance of homemade potpourris.

Best climate and site Zones 6–10. Thrives in poor, well-drained soil in full sun and tolerates drought.

Ideal soil conditions Poor, light, well-drained soil.

Growing guidelines Sow seed outdoors in spring where you want the plants to grow, then thin them to 1 foot (30 cm) apart. Or sow several seeds in pots several months before the last frost in a warm (70°F [21°C]) room. Transplants poorly. Stake or grow in clumps to prevent sprawling.

Growing habit Annual/biennial; height up to 2 feet (60 cm); its lacy foliage resembles Queen Anne's lace.

Flowering time Summer; dainty white, starlike blossoms in umbels.

Pest and disease prevention Anise oil is said to have insect-repellent properties; the strong smell of the plant may repel aphids and fleas.

Harvesting and storing Seeds are ready to harvest when they fall easily from the head. Clip off the seed heads into a bag before the seedpods shatter, but leave a few on the plant so it will self-sow for next year. Dry seeds on sheets of paper for several sunny days outdoors, then pasteurize in oven at 100°F (38°C) for 15 minutes

Licorice-scented anise seeds and the small white flowers of the anise plant can be dried and added to potpourris.

and store in airtight containers. Snip foliage as needed. The seeds can be used to flavor candy, pastry, cheese and biscotti. An infusion of vermouth and anise flowers is used to flavor muscatel wine.

Special tips Some companion gardeners say that a planting of anise will encourage coriander to germinate better and grow more vigorously. The strong smell of anise may repel aphids and fleas. An attractive pairing is made by a planting of creeping thyme at the feet of the anise plant. Some companion gardeners say that it may be detrimental to carrots.

LACY ANISE
Like other plants of the carrot family, anise produces lacy umbels of summer flowers that attract parasitic wasps and other beneficial insects to your garden.

ARNICA

Arnica montana Compositae

Arnica is a perennial with several flower stalks.
An ointment to soothe sprains, bruises and aching
muscles can be made using the flowers.

Best climate and site Zones
5–9. Prefers full sun but tolerates
light shade.

Ideal soil conditions Dry,
sandy soil with some humus.

Growing guidelines Sow seed
indoors in early spring; wait until
after the danger of frost before
transplanting outdoors. Propagate
by dividing the whole plant any
time in spring.

Growing habit Height to 2 feet
(60 cm); bright green leaves that
form a flat rosette, from the
center of which rises a flower
stalk. The rhizome is dark brown,

DRY WEATHER FLOWERS
While arnica generally grows best
with an even supply of moisture,
it will produce abundant, healthy
flowers in drier soil.

cylindrical, usually curved, and bears brittle, wiry rootlets on the under surface.

Flowering time Midsummer; yellow-orange daisy-like blossoms 2–3 inches (5–7.5 cm) across.

Pest and disease prevention Occasionally bothered by aphids. To control the pests, spray tops and bottoms of leaves with water. Dust or spray severe infestations with a botanical insecticide, like pyrethrin or derris.

Harvesting and storing Cut flowers from the stalk after they've dried. In autumn, dig roots after the leaves have died. Mix flowers with some vegetable oil or lard to make an ointment for aching muscles and for bruises.

Other common names Mountain tobacco, Leopard's Bane.

Precautions Use externally only. It can cause increased heart rate, nervous disturbances, vomiting and weakness. Arnica can also cause dermatitis in allergy-prone individuals. It works by stimulating the activity of white blood cells that perform much of the digestion of congested blood, and by dispersing trapped, disorganized fluids from bumped and bruised tissue, joints and muscles. It is known to stimulate blood circulation and can raise blood pressure, especially in the coronary arteries. Because it is a stimulant it should be used cautiously until a tolerance has been established.

WONDER HERB
Commercially prepared arnica creams and ointments are typically rubbed on the skin to soothe and heal bruises and sprains, and relieve irritations from trauma, arthritis and muscle or cartilage pain. Applied as a salve, arnica is also good for chapped lips, irritated nostrils and acne.

BASIL, SWEET

Ocimum basilicum Labiatae

Sweet basil is one of the most popular herbs in home gardens, mainly due to its strong flavor (with hints of licorice and pepper), which is so useful in the kitchen.

Fresh basil leaves are the basis of pesto and add flavor to summer salads.

Best climate and site Zones 6–10, but needs a sheltered site in the colder areas. Thrives on heat and full sun.

Ideal soil conditions Accepts a wide range of soil textures; likes rich, moist soil.

Growing guidelines Sow seed outdoors, after all danger of frost has passed, to a depth of about ⅛ inch (3 mm), then thin to 6 inches (15 cm). Or sow indoors in seed trays in warmth, six weeks before last frost, then transplant to small pots before setting outdoors. Mulch with compost to retain soil moisture, and prune away flowers to maintain best foliage flavor. Side-dress with compost in midseason to enhance production. Basil is easily damaged by low temperatures. In fall, cover with cloths to prolong the season and protect from the earliest frosts.

Growing habit Annual; height 1–2 feet (30–60 cm), width up to 18 inches (45 cm).

Flowering time Continuous beginning in midsummer; white blooms, carried in leafy spikes.

Pest and disease prevention Plant away from mint to prevent damage from plant bugs.

BASIL VARIETY
The most common basil is the brightly colored sweet basil with its intense scent and flavor. There are many cultivars ranging widely in color, size and aroma.

Harvesting and storing

Harvest leaves every week, pinching terminal buds first to encourage branching. The leaves can be used fresh or dried. The dried foliage loses its color and flavor but can be used as a tea to aid digestion; use one teaspoon of leaf per cup of water. Best preserved chopped and frozen, or as pesto. If freezing pesto, leave out the garlic until you're ready to use it, as garlic has a tendency to become bitter after a few months. Basil keeps well in a glass jar covered with olive oil.

Other common names

St. Josephwort.

COLORED RUFFLE

Purple ruffles basil is excellent in vinegar and as a garnish. It is also a striking ornamental.

SIMILAR SORTS

Green ruffles basil is an annual with leafy stems and thin branchy roots. It has the same culinary uses as sweet basil but is more delicate to grow.

Special tips Plant near tomatoes and peppers to enhance their growth. Some gardeners plant a second crop to ensure a plentiful supply when older plants become woody.

Cultivars The many different cultivars range widely in foliage size, color, aroma and plant habit.

❖ Anise basil (*O. basilicum 'Anise'*): Height to 4 feet (1.2 m); leaves have a sweet licorice scent; seed heads are a medium purple-red; easy to grow.

❖ Bush basil (*O. basilicum 'Minimum'*): Dwarf, bushy, compact, globe-like form; white flowers and small green leaves; grows well in pots.

❖ Dark opal basil (*O. basilicum 'Purpurascens'*): Lavender blossoms and deep purple, shiny foliage; poor germination.

❖ Lemon basil (*O. basilicum 'Citriodorum'*): Flowers and foliage with a lemony fragrance; whole plant and leaves smaller and more compact than sweet basil.

❖ Purple ruffles basil (*O. basilicum 'Purple Ruffles'*): Slow-growing, delicate seedlings. Plant early indoors in pots to minimize disturbance; do not over-water.

In order to release their essential oils, crush dried basil leaves in your hands before adding them to the pot.

BAY, SWEET

Laurus nobilis Lauraceae

Bay leaf garlands represent victory and accomplishment. Use the leaves for flavor in stews and soups, and as an aromatic addition to potpourri and herbal wreaths.

The fresh bay leaf is fragrant and leathery.

Use within a few days of drying for optimum flavor.

Best climate and site Zones 7–9, but needs a sheltered site in colder areas. Full sun to partial shade. Protect from wind.

Ideal soil conditions Rich, moist well-drained soil.

Growing guidelines Take cuttings from fresh green shoots in fall and keep the soil in which you plant them moist, since rooting may take three to nine months. In warm climates, sow seed outdoors; germination may require six to twelve months. Grows well in pots if moved indoors during frosty spells indoors; survives moderate frost in the garden. Trim away roots from large, pot-bound plants and add fresh compost to stimulate new growth.

Growing habit Evergreen tree; height up to 60 feet (18 m) but kept to desired size with pruning.

Flowering time Spring; inconspicuous, yellowish flowers; rarely flowers in containers.

Pest and disease prevention Mainly trouble-free. Dried leaves sprinkled in kitchen cupboards repel storage pests.

Harvesting and storing Best used fresh but the leathery leaves can be dried and stored in airtight jars.

Special tips Add whole leaves to soups and stews at the beginning of recipes, since bay holds its flavor a long time in cooking. Remove before serving as the leaf can be bitter.

MEDICINAL BAY
Bay is the only of the laurels that is not poisonous. It can be infused as a digestive aid and blended with essential oil for massage into rheumatic joints.

BERGAMOT

Monarda didyma Labiatae

This North American native has a citrusy fragrance and brilliant blooms in a range of colors. A tea of infused bergamot was a popular drink in New England after the Boston Tea Party in 1773.

Best climate and site Zones 6–9. Likes full sun but tolerates partial shade.

Ideal soil conditions Rich, moist, humusy soil.

Growing guidelines Grow from seed, cuttings or division. Plants grown from seed flower in the second year. Divide established plants every three years and discard old growth. For autumn blooms, prune stems to 6 inches (15 cm) after first flowering.

Growing habit Perennial; height 3–4 feet (90–120 cm) in line-forming, spreading clumps about the same width.

DRIED DECOR

The fresh flowers make a colorful bouquet. The dried flowers and leaves retain their color well, so they are a good addition to potpourris.

Flowering time Summer for several weeks; tubular flowers clustered together with bracts ranging in color from red and pink to lavender and white.

Pest and disease prevention Plant away from mint, since it attracts the same insect pests. Prune after flowering to discourage foliage diseases.

Harvesting and storing Harvest leaves for tea just before blooming and dry them quickly for best flavor. Pull individual flowers for a fresh salad garnish. Dry flowers with stems in bunches of five or six, then add to wreaths and arrangements.

Bergamot is used to relieve nausea and insomnia.

HEADY GROWTH
Bergamot plants attract butterflies and bumblebees. Support may be needed if the plants become top-heavy.

Special tips Plant near tomatoes or peppers to enhance their health and growth. Bergamot attracts bumble bees but not honeybees which cannot reach the nectar unless holes have been made in the flower by other insects.

Other common names Bee balm, Oswego tea.

Other species ❖ Dotted mint (*M. punctata*): Annual, biennial or perennial; height to 3 feet (90 cm); also called horsemint.
❖ Lemon mint (*M. citriodora*): Annual or biennial; height to 2 feet (60 cm); 2 inches (5 cm) long, lance-shaped leaves; flowers spring to summer.

BIRCH

Betula spp. Betulaceae

Birch is an elegant tree with a delightful fragrance after rain. The twigs, inner bark and sap of birch trees are used as the main ingredient in birch beer, and the leaves can be used to make tea.

Best climate and site Zones 3–8. Full sun to partial shade.

Ideal soil conditions Fertile, ideally neutral to acid soil with good drainage.

Growing guidelines Sow seed when ripe in late summer or fall. Indoors, sow thickly in trays, cover only lightly, and keep moist. Transplant seedlings when about one year old into nursery rows outdoors. After two to three years, plant into permanent positions during spring or fall. Plant with plenty of room for the roots.

Growing habit Height to 90 feet (27 m); deciduous trees that live for 50–100 years, and sometimes more, depending on the growing conditions and climate.

Flowering time Spring; on the same tree, female catkins are small and cylindrical, and male catkins are longer, have a yellowish tinge and are pendulous.

ANCIENT BARK
Long ago the soft wood of the birch tree was used for roofs and to build boats. The bark provided writing material and medication.

Pest and disease prevention
Provide ample water during the summer months to keep birch trees free from pests and diseases. Watch for borers on the young, sappy limbs.

Harvesting and storing In spring, collect the sap by boring holes in the trunk, inserting a tube and collecting the liquid in a container. Collect leaves in spring and use them fresh, or dry and store them in an airtight container. Collect bark as it peels off the tree; dry the bark and twigs in a cool, dry area; store in airtight containers; keeps well. A tea of birch leaves can be used for the relief of gout and rheumatism.

SCALY FLOWERS
The elegant birch, with its silvery bark and oval leaves, produces male and female flowers that have scales instead of petals, which are called catkins.

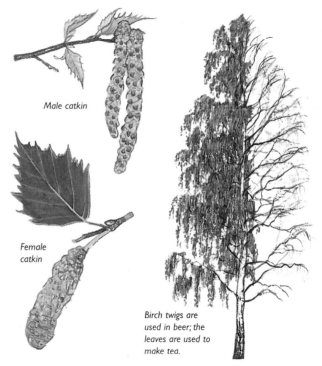

Male catkin

Female catkin

Birch twigs are used in beer; the leaves are used to make tea.

BORAGE

Borago officinalis Boraginaceae

This green, robust and bristly plant contrasts nicely with dark greens in the garden. The drooping clusters of blossoms attract honeybees, and the leaves have a cucumber flavor.

Best climate and site Zones 6–10. Prefers full sun but tolerates partial shade.

Ideal soil conditions Fairly rich, moist soil with good drainage.

Growing guidelines Sow seed ½ inch (1 cm) deep outdoors after danger of hard frost. Indoors, plant in pots to avoid disturbing the sensitive taproot when transplanting. Control weeds to reduce competition for moisture. To promote blooming, go easy on the nitrogen. Self-sows well. Tall plants may need support.

Growing habit
Annual; height 1½–2 feet (45–60 cm), width up to 18 inches (45 cm) with broad, hairy leaves arising from a central stalk.

BLUE STARS
The star-shaped flowers have five petals and come in shades of mauve through to bright blue.

Flowering time Continuously from midsummer until first frost; star-shaped circles of pink, purple, lavender or blue, with black centers.

Pest and disease prevention Mulch with light materials like straw to keep foliage off soil and prevent rotting.

Harvesting and storing Harvest foliage anytime and use raw, steamed or sautéed. Snip blossoms just after they open and candy, toss fresh in a salad or dry with silica gel for flower arrangements.

Precautions Some sources suggest that borage is toxic when consumed in large quantities over long periods of time.

THE HAPPY HERB
Historically, borage has the reputation of making people happy and giving them courage.

CALENDULA

Calendula officinalis Compositae

Calendula is a cheery, dependable bloomer in the garden. It is one of the most versatile herbs, with uses in cosmetic and culinary recipes, medicinal preparations, dyes and long-lasting fresh and dried bouquets.

Calendula flowers radiate from a pronounced center.

Calendula creams and ointments are available commercially.

Best climate and site Zones 6–10. Best in full sun but some shade is tolerated.

Ideal soil conditions Average garden soil with good drainage. Cannot tolerate waterlogged soil.

Growing guidelines Sow seed outdoors in fall or spring; thin to 10–18 inches (25–45 cm). Work in compost or aged manure before planting. Pinch away old blooms for continuous flowering.

Growing habit Annual; height 1–2 feet (30–60 cm); branched, succulent stem with fine hairs; leaves with hairy base.

Flowering time Summer; golden yellow

to orange flowers, 2–3 inches (5–7.5 cm) across.

Pest and disease prevention
Usually free from pests and diseases.

Harvesting and storing Dry petals in shade on paper to prevent sticking; store in moisture-proof jars. Preserve whole flowers in salad vinegar. Dried, ground calendula flowers can be used as a substitute for saffron.

Special tips Plant calendula seed in pots in July for indoor autumn color.

Other common names Pot marigold.

ORANGE POWER
Calendula oil has antiseptic properties. It's made from the brightest orange petals which have the highest concentration of active ingredients.

CARAWAY

Carum carvi Umbelliferae

The seeds of this annual or biennial have been used for 5,000 years for flavoring food and for their carminative effect. The seeds are also aromatic and can be used in potpourris.

Best climate and site Zones 6–10. Ideally in full sun.

Ideal soil conditions Fertile, light garden soil.

Growing guidelines Sow seed shallowly outdoors as early as the soil can be worked through to early fall, or indoors in pots; thin to 6–12 inches (15–30 cm). Sow seed outdoors for early spring plants or grow indoors in a sunny position. Don't allow seedlings to dry out, as they will not recover. The thick, long taproot makes transplanting difficult.

Growing habit Height 1–2 feet (30–60 cm); glossy, fine dissected foliage resembling the carrot plant; slender, branching stem; two narrow, brown seeds grow in each capsule, which bursts when ripe.

Flowering time Early summer

of the second year if sown in the fall; late summer if spring sown; white or pink flowers in umbels on stalks.

Pest and disease prevention Caraway is susceptible to many of the same pests and diseases as carrots, so it may be best to keep these two crops on separate sides of the vegetable garden; watch for pests in dried, stored seeds.

Harvesting and storage Snip tender leaves in spring and use fresh in salads, soups and stews.

The highly aromatic seeds are used in cooking, herbal craft and aromatherapy.

After blooming, cut plants when seeds are brown and almost loose, then hang them upside down in paper bags to dry. Collect seeds and dry a few more days in the sun; store in a tightly sealed container. The roots can be cooked in the same manner as any other root vegetable.

Special tips Excessive pruning during the first year weakens the plant. Caraway is a good companion to peas. It is slow to germinate, but if sown with fast-maturing peas, caraway seedlings will fill in after you harvest the peas. It has been observed that caraway does not grow well next to fennel.

ATTRACTIVE COMPANION
The tiny flowers of the caraway attract a multitude of insects, including predatory wasps and other beneficials.

CATMINT

Nepeta cataria Labiatae

Catmint is closely related to mint and is similarly hardy. If you plant catnip in the vegetable garden, be prepared to pull out self-sown seedlings and creeping shoots to control its spread, or grow it in an unused area.

Best climate and site Zones 6–9. Full sun to partial shade.

Ideal soil conditions Dry, sandy garden soil.

Growing guidelines Sow seed outdoors when ripe or in early spring; thin to 18 inches (45 cm). Take cuttings in early summer.

Growing habit Height 1–3 feet (30–90 cm); new stems each season from a perennial root; heart-shaped, toothed, grayish green leaves.

Flowering time Summer to early fall bloomer; white, purple dotted flowers in branching spikes.

USEFUL LEAVES

The leaves and flowering top of the catmint plant contain vitamin C. Dried, the leaves retain their mintlike scent but have a sharp taste.

Pest and disease prevention
Usually free from pests and diseases; planting near susceptible

With its lavender-blue flowers, catmint makes an attractive edging plant.

plants such as eggplants and turnips appears to reduce infestations of flea beetles. Catmint can, however, carry cucumber mosaic virus, a problem on most crops of the squash family. The vapor also chases away spittlebugs, ants, Japanese beetles, weevils and a dozen other species.

Harvesting and storing In late summer, strip topmost leaves from stems and spread them to dry on a screen in the shade, or hang bunches upside down. Store in tightly sealed containers. Make a tea from the dried leaves to use as a carminative, tonic and mild sedative. Use fresh leaves in salads.

Special tips Bruise a few leaves and leave them near your cat's food. The scent that is released will make him feel

Grow catmint in pots to contain the aggressive spread.

like a playful kitten. The pretty purple blooms are good fillers in fresh arrangements and contrast well with white flowers.

CAYENNE PEPPER

Capsicum annuum Solanaceae

Peppers are heat-lovers, so don't set plants out too early. Or use a heating cable, which is sold at garden centers or in catalogs, for this purpose; you may also have success by placing the tray of pots on top of your refrigerator!

Dry peppers whole, or chop and freeze them in zippered plastic bags.

Best climate and site Zones 8–10. Greenhouse or very sheltered borders out of doors in full sun in cooler areas.

Ideal soil conditions Well-manured moist soil.

Growing guidelines Seeds are slow to germinate, often waiting a month to make an appearance. Sow seed in warmth; set young plants outdoors several weeks after last frost. Plant 12–18 inches (30–45 cm) apart in 30-inch (75-cm) rows.

A very hot, biting condiment is made from the dried seeds and pods.

Growing habit Height 1–2 feet (30–60 cm); shrubby tropical perennial, grown as an annual.

Flowering time Midsummer; flowers followed by red, orange or yellow fruit. Protect the blossoms from sun and wind damage by planting with taller plants.

Pest and disease prevention

Pests tend to avoid these spicy plants. However it's best to keep peppers away from beans; both are susceptible to anthracnose, a disease that causes dark, soft spots on fruits. Weed regularly; related weeds such as deadly nightshade and groundcherries may be carriers of mosaic virus.

Harvesting and storing

When fruits are uniformly red, cut them from the plant, leaving stem at least ½ inch (1 cm) long. Dry them immediately on screens, or string them together using a needle and heavy thread. Or pull and hang the whole plant to dry. Store peppers whole or ground in tightly sealed containers.

AIDING GROWTH

A dose of fish emulsion when plants are in flower can help increase yields.

CHAMOMILE, ROMAN
Chamaemelum nobile Compositae

Herb gardens of yesterday often included a lush lawn of chamomile that released a sweet, apple-like scent when walked upon. The tea is relaxing after a stressful day.

Best climate and site Zones 6–9. Full sun to partial shade.

Ideal soil conditions Light, moist but well-drained garden soil.

Growing guidelines Sow seed indoors or outdoors; thin seedlings to 6 inches (15 cm). Once firmly established, it can self-sow. Divide older plants in early spring. In the first year, clip to prevent flowering and encourage vegetative growth while it becomes established. Creeping rootstock spreads the plant, creating a carpet-like surface. Established lawns can be mowed like grass. Chamomile is a poor competitor, so weed often.

PRETTY COMPANION
The white daisies and ferny foliage have a fresh smell of apple, which attracts many beneficial insects, like hover flies and wasps.

Growing habit Height 6–9 inches (15–23 cm); low-growing perennial with aromatic, lacy foliage.

Flowering time Summer; white, daisy-like flowers with yellow centers.

Pest and disease prevention Usually free from pests and diseases.

Harvesting and storing Collect flowers at full bloom and dry on screens or paper. Store in tightly sealed containers.

HERBAL HEALTH
Roman chamomile is commercially prepared as a treatment for many medical conditions. The dried flowers make a soothing tea.

Other common names Garden chamomile, ground apple, Russian chamomile. German chamomile (*Matricaria recutita*) has similar flowers but grows much taller and is an annual.

German chamomile

CHERVIL
Anthriscus cerefolium Umbelliferae

Chervil grows best, and retains more flavor, when temperatures are low, in spring and fall. Grow this lacy, delicate-looking plant for medicinal, culinary, cosmetic and craft uses.

Best climate and site Zones 6–10. Full sun or shade.

Ideal soil conditions Moist, well-drained, humusy garden soil.

Growing guidelines Sow fresh seed shallowly outdoors in early spring or fall; thin to 9–12 inches (23–30 cm); keep seedlings moist. Sow again at two-week intervals until mid-July for continuous harvest. Transplants poorly. Mulch to protect autumn-sown seeds. Chervil can seed itself each year if flowers are left to mature in the garden. Seed can be collected in the fall for a spring crop the next year.

Growing habit Annual; height 1–2 feet (30–60 cm); fernlike leaves.

Flowering time Summer; small umbrella-like, white clusters.

Pest and disease prevention Usually free from pests and diseases.

Harvesting and storing Snip leaves continuously after six to

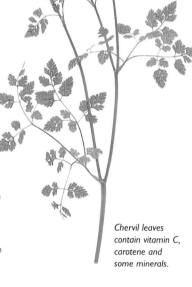

Chervil leaves contain vitamin C, carotene and some minerals.

eight weeks; best used fresh. The warm pungency of chervil—like a combination of anise and parsley—is good in soups and salads. The leaves are often included with parsley, thyme and tarragon in French cooking.

Special tips Chervil loses flavor quickly when heated, so add to recipes at the end. Chervil grows well below taller plants that offer some shade. Some companion gardeners recommend planting chervil with radishes to improve their flavor.

Other common names Garden chervil.

BORDER PLANT
Chervil bears heads of tiny white flowers that attract beneficial insect predators and parasites to the garden. Grow it as a border or interplant it with your vegetables.

CHICORY

Cichorium intybus Compositae

Look for chicory's bright blue flowers along roadsides and field edges. This hardy, wild plant thrives under a variety of harsh conditions; it doesn't like the cosy warmth of indoors.

Best climate and site Zones 6–9. Full sun.

Ideal soil conditions Average to poor, deeply tilled, well-drained garden soil.

Growing guidelines Sow the seed outdoors in spring, thinning to 1 foot (30 cm). Side-dress in midsummer with compost or rotted manure, but avoid heavy nitrogen applications. Keep weeded and moist. In the autumn, plants can be forced indoors away from light to produce chicons. To do this, plant roots trimmed to 8–9 inches (20–23 cm) long in deep containers and keep away

CHANGING COLOR

The clear blue flowers change to bright red if affected by the acid of ants. The plant is used in floral clocks because of the regular opening of the flowers, and their closing five hours later.

from light. Within about three weeks, cone-shaped heads of leaves 6 inches (15 cm) long are ready to be sliced off and used. Discard the root and start again with a new one.

Growing habit Deep-rooted perennial with bristly, branched stem. If not harvested, flowering stems reach a height of 3–5 feet (90–150 cm).

The dried, ground roots can be used as a coffee substitute.

Flowering time Early spring to fall; bright blue dandelion-shaped flowers open and close each morning and evening, even when cut for arrangements.

Pest and disease prevention Few pests bother this fast-grower.

Harvesting and storing Use leaves fresh in salads or cook like spinach. Chicory leaves do not dry or freeze well. Collect the roots in the fall, and dry and grind them for a coffee substitute. When the roots are young, they can be boiled and served with a sauce. The chicons, which are sometimes referred to as Belgian endives, can be braised and served as a vegetable dish.

COLOR POWER
The dried petals are attractive in potpourri, and the leaves can be boiled to make a blue dye.

CHIVES

Allium schoenoprasum Liliaceae

The graceful leaves and blossoms have a mild onion flavor, especially when used fresh. Use the leaves in cooking and toss the flowers in salads or use them as a garnish.

Best climate and site Zones 6–9. Full sun.

Ideal soil conditions Rich, well-drained soil.

Growing guidelines Sow seed indoors in late winter, covering the seeds lightly and keeping the soil moist; transplant in clumps in early spring; space 5–8 inches (12–20 cm) apart. Sow outside in spring. Every three years, divide older clumps in the early spring and freshen with compost.

Growing habit Height 6–12 inches (15–30 cm); perennial bulb with green, tubular leaves.

HANDY POTS

Chives are pretty enough to make an attractive container planting. Keep the pot near the kitchen so you can snip off the leaves as you need them.

Chinese chives

Chives

Flowering time June; pink or lavender to purple globular flower heads.

Pest and disease prevention Avoid wet areas that encourage stem and bulb diseases.

Harvesting and storing Use fresh leaf tips all summer once the plants are 6 inches (15 cm) tall; leave at least 2 inches (5 cm) remaining. Chives are best used fresh, or chopped and dried. They freeze poorly.

Special tips Chives are recommended companion plants for carrots, grapes, roses and tomatoes because they ward off Japanese beetles and black spot. A ring of chives around an apple tree may inhibit the growth of apple scab (possibly by affecting the

STOPPING THE SPREAD
It's best to pinch off the spent flowers if you want to prevent self-sowing.

spores carried on dropped leaves). Some companion gardeners believe that chives inhibit the growth of beans or peas.

Other species ❖ Chinese chives (*A. tuberosum*): The flowers are white and the leaves are flat, broader and larger. They have a garlicky aroma and flavor, so they are sometimes called garlic chives.

Easy-to-grow chives add pretty pink or purple blossoms to the garden.

CLARY
Salvia sclarea Labiatae

Fresh clary, also known as clary sage, is an attractive flowering garden plant that keeps its flavor in cooking, provides a soothing scent in potpourris and produces an essential oil that has many uses in herbal medicines.

Best climate and site Zones 6–9. Full sun.

Ideal soil conditions Average, well-drained soil.

Growing guidelines Sow seed outdoors in spring; thin to around 9 inches (23 cm). Can be propagated by division of two-year-old plants in early spring or fall, but is best raised from seed annually.

Growing habit Biennial or short-lived perennial; height 2–5 feet (60–150 cm); upright, branched, square stems with broad, oblong aromatic leaves.

Flowering time June to July after first year; small, pale blue to lavender blossoms resemble garden sage.

Pest and disease prevention Usually free from pests and diseases.

Harvesting and storing Snip leaves for fresh use. Strip leaves and dry them on screens for use in herbal craft. The oil is distilled from the flowering tops.

Special tips Clary has a sweet, nutty scent. Use in potpourris with scents such as juniper, lavender, cardomon, citrus, geranium, pine, bergamot, frankincense, coriander, sandalwood, cedarwood and jasmine. The essential oil is a complex mix of elements and is thought to have a particular affinity with the female cycle. It can be used in a massage oil or in a compress for the relief of muscular cramps, aches and pains, as well as indigestion. Clary is also

Clary essential oil is generally produced from plants grown in France, Morocco and England. The oil is colorless or a pale yellow-green.

thought to have antiseptic properties which make it beneficial for skin infections and viruses. The oil is used commercially as a fragrance component and fixative in soaps, detergents, cosmetics and in many perfumes. It's also used extensively by the food and beverage industry, especially in wine production.

Precautions Clary sage oil may cause drowsiness and must not be used when consuming alcohol or by anyone suffering from epilepsy. It should also be avoided in all forms during pregnancy, or if you have any medical conditions affected by the hormone estrogen.

RELAXING SCENT
The soothing, sweet scent of clary has traditionally been used in gardens designed for relaxation. Plant it near garden seats or along a path.

COFFEE
Coffea arabica Rubiaceae

Coffee beans are actually the seeds, inside a pulpy fruit. To produce the seeds, the plant requires a hot, moist climate and rich soil. In cool climates, coffee can be grown as an ornamental in pots.

Best climate and site Zones 9–10 or greenhouse with a minimum winter temperature of 55–60°F (13–16°C).

Ideal soil conditions Humusy, well-drained soil.

Growing guidelines Sow seed shallowly in spring in a temperature of not less than 65°F (18°C). Does well indoors in pots, but benefits from regular misting with water to maintain humidity.

Growing habit Height 15–20 feet (4.5–6 m); large shrub or evergreen tree.

ESSENTIAL FLAVOR
The mature, red fruit of the coffee plant (called a drupe) usually contains two seeds, or coffee beans. The harvested seeds are cleaned and roasted; heat acts on the essential oils to produce the aroma and flavor.

Roasts range from light brown to the very dark Italian roast.

Special tips Most commercial brands of coffee are actually a blend of several different types. Coffee contains caffeine, which is a stimulant that can cause irritability, depression and indigestion if taken in excess. Varieties of Arabian coffee supply the bulk of the world's supply.

Flowering time Late spring; white, star-shaped blooms in clusters, followed by deep red berries which contain two large seeds, the beans of commerce.

Pest and disease prevention For healthy plants, keep coffee well watered during periods of dry weather.

Harvesting and storing Collect the berries when they are deep red, and extract the seeds. Sun dry for seven to ten days, then roast them.

ANCIENT STORY
The coffee plant was known before AD 1000 in Ethiopia, where its fruit was used for food and wine. A beverage made from ground, roasted coffee beans was used in Arabia by the 15th century and by the mid-17th century it had reached most of Europe and had been introduced into North America.

COMFREY

Symphytum officinale Boraginaceae

Comfrey is an attractive plant with large, broad, deep green leaves and nodding clusters of tubular flowers. It is grown more for its ornamental and medicinal value than for its culinary uses.

Best climate and site Zones 6–9. Full sun to partial shade.

Ideal soil conditions Rich, moist garden soil.

Growing guidelines Propagate by seed, division or cuttings; space new plants 3 feet (90 cm) apart. Establishes easily and requires little care; remove dead leaves during fall cleanup. Divide every few years to prevent crowding.

Growing habit Height 2–4 feet (60–120 cm); new leaves sprout each spring from a perennial root.

Flowering time Early to late summer; terminal cluster of purple pink, white or cream flowers.

Pest and disease prevention Usually free from diseases and pests, though it is worth checking.

Harvesting and storing Pinch the leaves from the stems and use them fresh or dry. Leaves for drying are best picked in spring. The roots should be unearthed in spring or fall. Split the roots down the middle and dry in moderate temperatures on screens or in the oven. Store leaves and roots in airtight containers; use them in a salve or compress to treat external bruises, wounds, ulcers and sores.

Special tips Shaded plants will be smaller, with few blossoms. Comfrey is high in potassium, vitamin A and calcium, and contains a mucilage that helps in healing. It should, however, only be used direct from the garden in external applications. For internal use, commercially processed comfrey is suggested for cleansing the blood and repairing tissue.

Comfrey gel soothes bruises and can be effective on slow-healing sores.

Precautions Comfrey is a suspected carcinogen; take internally only in a commercially prepared form. If used excessively or for longer than three months, it may cause liver damage. Pregnant and nursing women should consult a healthcare professional.

Other common names
Knitbone, slippery root, bruisewort and boneset.

HAIRY LEAVES
The leaves of the comfrey plant are long and covered on the top surface by many short hairy bristles. The leaves appear to be stacked one upon the other, larger at the base than at the top, forming a large clump. The drooping, bell-shaped flowers are blue, white, purple or pale yellow, depending on the species.

CORIANDER

Coriandrum sativum Umbelliferae

Coriander is a dainty annual plant with finely divided leaves that are both strong-smelling and tasting. Its seeds, which become more fragrant with age, are popular ingredients in the kitchen and in potpourri.

Best climate and site
Zones 6–10. Ideally full sun, but some shade tolerated.

Ideal soil conditions
Moderately rich, well-drained soil.

Growing guidelines
Sow seed ½ inch (1 cm) deep outdoors after danger of frost, or in fall; thin to 4 inches (10 cm). Can self-sow. Weed diligently to prevent delicate seedlings from being overcome by more vigorous weeds. To prevent sprawling, avoid heavy applications of nitrogen.

The roots are used in salsa and curries.

STRONG SCENT
Coriander was named after the bedbug emitting the same odor! It adds a strong fragrance to the garden.

Growing habit Annual; height 1–3 feet (30–90 cm); graceful, glossy, finely dissected foliage resembles Queen Anne's lace.

Flowering time Early to late summer, depending on when sown; tiny white flowers in umbels.

Pest and disease prevention Usually free from pests and diseases.

Coriander seeds have a delicious perfumed taste and deep color.

Harvesting and storing Harvest foliage before seeds form and use fresh. Dried foliage is of lesser quality. Freezes poorly. Gather the seeds as they ripen in midsummer. Contains some anti-bacterial and anti-fungal properties and has been used for preserving meats. Also has anti-inflammatory properties and may be helpful for arthritis, muscle and joint pain.

Special tips Sow every two to three weeks for a continuous supply of fresh leaves. Grown near anise, coriander helps the seeds germinate, but grown near fennel, it hinders germination. It grows well with chervil. Honeybees are attracted to the flowers. The seeds remain viable for five to seven years. Looks attractive against borage and bee balm.

Other common names Cilantro, Chinese parsley.

PRETTY IN POTS
Coriander is easily grown from seed sown in spring. It does well in containers with good soil. The leaves can be picked sparingly as needed for culinary use. In pots, coriander makes a good ornamental with its small white or purplish-tinged flowers.

COSTMARY

Chrysanthemum balsamita Compositae

In the summer, enjoy costmary's mint-scented leaves in your garden. In the fall, harvest whole stems for weaving into fragrant herb baskets. Small amounts, finely chopped, can be added to soups, stews and poultry dishes.

Best climate and site Zones 6–9. Full sun, though some shade tolerated.

Ideal soil conditions Well-drained, fertile, loamy soil.

Growing guidelines Plants produce little or no seed, so propagate by dividing older plants in spring. Space at 2 feet (60 cm) intervals. Divide plants every two to three years, since they spread quickly. Avoid shade, since costmary will not flower without sun. For more foliage production, discourage flowering by pruning away buds.

Growing habit Height 1–3 feet (60–90 cm); perennial roots with large, green to silvery, hairy foliage.

FOLIAGE ONLY
Grown in the shade, costmary goes strongly to leaf, but will not flower.

Flowering time Late summer, but may not bloom; flowers very small or absent.

Pest and disease prevention Usually disease- and pest-free.

Harvesting and storing Collect leaves and dry as needed. To harvest foliage for baskets, harvest whole stems in late summer or fall and hang to dry.

Special tips Add fresh leaves to salads for a minty flavor, or add dried leaves to potpourri.

Other common names Alecost, mace.

SWEET DREAMS
In days gone by, the fresh-scented blooms would be placed between bedsheets in the linen cupboard.

DANDELION

Taraxacum officinale Compositae

Some of us have learned to appreciate this brightly colored lawn pest. If your thumb is other than green, try planting dandelions to boost your self-confidence in the garden!

Dandelion is extremely high in iron and vitamin A.

Best climate and site Zones 5–9. Full sun to partial shade.

Ideal soil conditions Any moderately fertile soil. Keep constantly and evenly moist.

Growing guidelines It's best to obtain seeds of a large-leaved selection from a specialist seed catalogue and sow shallowly in early spring. For large roots that are easy to dig, work in plenty of compost or rotted manure to loosen the soil.

Growing habit Perennial; height 6–12 inches (15–30 cm); leaves jagged, arising from a basal rosette.

Flowering time Late spring; well-known golden yellow disks mature to puffballs of seeds.

Pest and disease prevention Usually disease- and pest-free.

HEADY GROWTH
Dandelion can become a problem in gardens if allowed to grow unchecked. Thin your plantings regularly.

Harvesting and storing Dig the roots in fall, and cut or slice them into small pieces, then air dry or roast in a slow oven. Use dried, roasted and ground roots to prepare a caffeine-free coffee substitute. Harvest young, fresh leaves for spring salads, soups and wine; less bitter if blanched first.

Dried dandelion root is a healthy coffee substitute.

DILL
Anethum graveolens Umbelliferae

Dill's tall, graceful habit makes it an attractive background in flower beds. In American history, dill seed was known as the meeting seed because it was given to children to induce sleep during long Sunday sermons.

Best climate and site Zones 6–10. Full sun.

Ideal soil conditions Rich, well-drained soil.

Growing guidelines In spring, sow seeds in shallow drills about 10 inches (25 cm) apart in a prepared bed, where they will stay. Firm the soil down and water well. Repeat the plantings for a continuous supply of fresh dill leaves. The soft, delicate seedlings do not transplant well and are easily blown over by strong winds. The plants do best in a sunny, sheltered area. Keep seedlings moist; weed diligently.

DILL PICKLES
Dill has a taproot like a carrot, with one long, hollow stalk coming from the root. The small stems and immature umbels are used for flavoring seafood sauces and making pickles.

The entire dill plant is aromatic. The ripened fruits are the pungent seed, while the leafy tops provide the more delicately scented dill weed.

Growing habit Height 2–3 feet (60–90 cm); hardy annual resembling fennel.

Flowering time Summer; yellowish flowers in umbels.

Pest and disease prevention Usually disease- and pest-free.

Harvesting and storing Clip fresh leaves at the stem as needed. They can be chopped finely for sauces or used whole as garnish. Freeze whole leaves, or chop first; or dry foliage on nonmetallic screens. Collect the flower heads before the seeds mature and fall; hang them in paper bags or dry them on paper. If stored in airtight containers, dill seed will retain its flavor for at least a year, but dill weed quickly loses its potency, even in good storage conditions. Fresh leaves can be refrigerated for one week at most.

POTTED COLOR
Grow dill in pots and move it around the garden to attract beneficials.

Special tips Sow seeds every two to three weeks for a continuous leaf harvest through to fall. Dill and cabbage plants grow well together. Companion gardeners also note that dill helps cucumbers, corn, lettuce and onions. The flowers attract honeybees to the garden.

143

DOCK, CURLED

Rumex crispus Polygonaceae

Curled dock is a perennial weed found in pastures and hayfields, on the roadside and in other non-tilled areas. Only the roots are edible and are used in medicines. The flowers are used in craft.

Best climate and site Zones 5–9. Full sun.

Ideal soil conditions Any soil with slightly acid pH.

Growing guidelines Sow seed in shallow beds in spring, then thin to 6 inches (15 cm). Weedy and hard to control, dock thrives despite neglect. Control its growth to prevent a future weed problem.

Growing habit Perennial; height 2–4 feet (60–120 cm); it forms a rosette the first year, then develops a large taproot and sends up a tall stem. From this central point come long, lance-shaped, wavy leaves. The flowers are inconspicuous but the seed capsule is rusty brown in the fall and is easily recognized. Each plant produces 3,000 to 4,000 seeds. As well as being a prolific breeder, dock is allelopathic; it keeps other kinds of plants from crowding in around it by releasing inhibitory chemicals into the soil or air to reduce competition for nutrients.

Flowering time June to August; small, greenish-yellow flowers in spreading panicles.

Pest and disease prevention Usually disease- and pest-free.

Harvesting and storing Dig roots in spring or fall; clean and slice them before drying in the sun or artificially. Store in a tightly sealed container. Drink an infusion of dried, ground dock as a laxative; use the infusion externally as an astringent tonic and to treat skin problems. Apply externally in a salve or compress for eczema, hives, nettle rash, boils, psoriasis and wounds. The flowers are good for dried wreaths or arrangements.

Special tips Most dock seed falls close to the parent. Soil movement may distribute seeds. Cultivation of the soil may damage the root and create root fragments, allowing new plants to form from each fragment. Docks can be very competitive in pastures and irrigated production areas, such as orchards. They can form large infestations and drastically reduce grazing capacity. They grow prolifically on dairy properties, especially in areas watered by washings from the dairy.

Other common names Yellow dock, narrow dock, sour dock and rumex. The name dock is applied to a widespread tribe of broad-leaved wayside weeds that have roots with astringent qualities. Although dock is now, in common with sorrels, assigned to the genus *Rumex*, dock used to be ranked as a member of the genus *Lapathum*, from the Greek word, *lapazein* (which means to cleanse).

NO APPEAL FOR THE SENSES
Dock has little or no smell and a rather bitter taste. It is similar in look to rhubarb and in flavor to sorrel.

ELECAMPANE

Inula helenium Compositae

Elecampane is a tall perennial with hairy stems and yellow, ragged flowers. It is grown for its root which, through the ages, has been candied as a confectionery and used for medicinal purposes.

Best climate and site Zones 6–9. Full sun to light shade.

Ideal soil conditions
Moderately fertile, moist soil.

Growing guidelines Sow seed outdoors in spring, or collect root cuttings from mature plants in fall; winter them in frame pots, setting plants out in the garden the following summer.

Growing habit Height 4–6 feet (120–180 cm); branched perennial with large, elliptical basal leaves and smaller, oblong top leaves.

GENTLE GIANT
Its stature and huge, soft leaves are the elecampane plant's most notable visual features, but it is not known as an ornamental. It's grown for its root, which is thick and black on the outside and white inside; it tastes bitter but has a gentle scent and healing properties.

Flowering time Summer months; daisy-like yellow flowers 3–4 inches (7–10 cm) across.

Pest and disease prevention Usually trouble-free. Vulnerable to pests that suck juices from leaves. Control with a botanical insecticide like pyrethrin.

Harvesting and storing Collect roots for medicinal and culinary use in the fall of the plant's second season, after several hard frosts. Dry them thoroughly before storing. The fresh roots, preserved with sugar, or made into a syrup or conserve, are very effective for stomachaches and respiratory problems. The dried root, made into powder, mixed with sugar and mixed into hot water, serves the same purpose. The distilled water of the boiled leaves and roots is good for all kinds of skin problems.

Special tips It is best propagated by offsets, taken in the fall from the old root, with a bud or eye to each. These will take root very readily, and should be planted in rows about a foot away from each other and with about a foot between the rows. In the following spring, the ground should be kept clean from weeds. Slight digging in the fall will greatly promote the development of the roots, which will be fit for use after two years.

Other common names Inula, inul, horseheal, elf dock, elfwort, horse elder, yellow starwort, velvet dock, cabwort and scabwort.

ADDING COLOR
The flowers will add color to your garden; they are bright yellow, in very large, terminal heads, about 4 inches (10 cm) in diameter, on long stalks, resembling a double sunflower.

147

EUCALYPTUS (BLUE GUM)

Eucalyptus globulus Myrtaceae

Eucalyptus are evergreen trees well known for their pungent scent and silvery leaves. They are often called fever trees, being largely cultivated in unhealthy, swampy districts for their antiseptic properties.

The first leaves are often broad, shiny and pale but are succeeded in a few years by long, bluish-green leaves.

Best climate and site Zones 9–10 or a frost-free greenhouse in cooler zones.

Ideal soil conditions Light, loamy soils; tolerates wide range of soil pH.

Growing guidelines Best to purchase young, potted trees, but can easily be grown from seed under glass.

Growing habit Over 500 species, ranging from 5 feet (1.5 m) shrubs to 300 feet (95 m) trees. The blue gum is the best known, with smooth blue-gray bark

ESSENTIAL USES
The oils are either medicinal, industrial (used for flotation purposes in mining operations) or aromatic.

and silvery blue leathery leaves, both of which have a camphor-like fragrance. Can reach over 100 feet (33 m) in a mild climate.

Flowering time Depends on species; most with umbel of flowers in white, cream, pink, yellow, orange or red.

Pest and disease prevention
Few severe pest problems. A spray made from blended eucalyptus foliage may deter garden pests.

Harvesting and storing
Leaves, branches and seedpods dry quickly for craft uses and retain their scent; oils can be extracted from some species.

POOR COMPANION
Silver dollar gum is suited to container growing and may be more useful in a pot because, like most eucalypts, it is detrimental to neighboring plants.

FENNEL

Foeniculum vulgare Umbelliferae

Grow licorice-scented fennel as a tall ornamental in the flower garden, and for its culinary uses in the kitchen. The leaves and seeds are also used in cosmetics and herbal medicines.

HERB OF MANY USES

Raw fennel seeds are thought to be an appetite suppressant; the essential oil is used as a fragrance in creams, perfumes, soaps, liqueurs and potpourris, and to medicate the skin and reduce swelling.

Fennel oil soothes bruises. Nibble on the raw seeds.

Best climate and site Zones 6–9. Full sun.

Ideal soil conditions Humusy, well-drained soil.

Growing guidelines Sow seed shallowly outdoors in spring or fall and keep moist; thin to 6 inches (15 cm); transplants poorly.

Growing habit Semi-hardy perennial usually grown as an annual; height to 4 feet (1.2 m); the leaves are feathery and blue-green in color.

Flowering time July to October; small, yellow flowers in umbels.

Pest and disease prevention Usually disease- and pest-free.

Harvesting and storing Snip leaves before blooming for fresh use; leaves can also be frozen.

Collect seeds when dry but before they shatter by snipping the ripe seed heads into a paper bag; dry them on paper.

Special tips Fennel's delicate flavor is destroyed by heat, so add at the end of the recipe. Try the bronze-colored variety for foliage contrast outdoors, and on the dinner plate as a garnish. Most companion gardeners keep fennel away from the vegetable garden, alleging that this licorice-scented herb inhibits the growth of bush beans, kohlrabi, tomatoes and other crops.

BORDER FLOWERS
Plant fennel in an ornamental border rather than in or near a vegetable garden. Its lacy leaves and airy flower heads combine well with flowering ornamentals. Wasps and other beneficials are attracted by the flowers.

FENUGREEK

Trigonella foenum-graecum Leguminosae

Fenugreek is a member of the same family as beans and clover. The seeds are used as a substitute for maple flavoring in baked goods and to make a laxative tea.

Best climate and site Zones 6–10. Full sun.

Ideal soil conditions Rich soil.

Growing guidelines When springtime soil temperatures reach 60°F (15°C), sow a thick band of seed outdoors, covering shallowly. Avoid growing in cold, wet soils, since seeds will rot before they can germinate. As a leguminous plant, fenugreek needs little if any nitrogen fertilizer, and the plant can enrich soils with nitrogen.

Growing habit Annual; height 1–2 feet (30–60 cm); clover-like stems and leaves.

ANCIENT HISTORY

Undoubtedly one of the oldest cultivated medicinal plants, fenugreek is widely grown today in the United States as a food, condiment, medicinal, dye and forage plant.

Flowering time Summer; white flowers with distinctive pink or blue markings that resemble garden pea blossoms.

Pest and disease prevention Snails and slugs can be a problem on new growth; the most effective remedy is to handpick the pests from the plants.

Harvesting and storing Harvest pods when ripe but before they fall, like garden beans; leave seeds in the sun to dry, then store in an airtight container. For culinary purposes, such as curries, the dried seeds can be ground and then stored. Young seedlings and other portions of the fresh plant can be eaten as vegetables. Fenugreek has a strong, pleasant, peculiar odor reminiscent of maple, which makes it useful in many baked goods, chutneys, preserves and confections.

Special tips Steep the seeds in boiling water and strain, for a substitute for maple syrup. Fenugreek can be used as a livestock feed. As a medicinal plant, fenugreek has traditionally been employed against bronchitis, fevers, sore throats, wounds swollen glands, skin irritations, diabetes and ulcers. Fenugreek seeds may also lower blood glucose levels. As a cover crop, fenugreek breaks up heavy soils and contributes nitrogen and organic matter. Marsh mallow and fenugreek is a time-honored herbal combination used to nutritionally support the respiratory system. The plant is quite nutritious, being high in proteins, ascorbic acid, niacin and potassium.

Other common names Bird's foot, Greek hay-seed; fenugreek was used in Mediterranean countries to scent inferior hay.

Precautions None; fenugreek is generally recognized as safe for human consumption as a spice or natural seasoning and as a plant extract in herbal medicines.

FURROWED SEEDS
The seeds are brownish, oblong, rhomboidal, with a deep furrow dividing them into two unequal lobes. They are contained, ten to twenty together, in long, narrow, sickle-like pods.

GARLIC

Allium sativum Liliaceae

Garlic is one of the most familiar herbs, used to flavor dishes from almost every ethnic group. Garlic is also often recommended by companion gardeners as an insect-repelling plant.

Its bulb is the best storage container for garlic.

Plant or use garlic cloves soon after separating them from the bulb.

HEALTHY GROWTH
The larger cloves produce the largest, and usually healthiest, bulbs.

Best climate and site Zones 6–10. Ideally in full sun.

Ideal soil conditions Humusy, deep, well-drained soil.

Growing guidelines Separate individual cloves from the bulb immediately before planting, then plant in October for harvesting the following summer; space 6 inches (15 cm) apart and 2 inches (5 cm) deep. For largest bulbs, prune away flowering stems that shoot up in early summer; side-dress with compost in early spring; avoid planting after heavy applications of fresh manure.

Growing habit Biennial or perennial; height to 2 feet (60 cm); foliage narrowly strap-shaped.

Flowering time Early summer; small, white to pinkish blooms atop a tall central stalk.

Pest and disease prevention
Avoid over-watering the soil to prevent bulb diseases.

Harvesting and storing Dig bulbs after tops have died down, and before bulb skins begin to decay underground; place in a single layer in a shaded spot to dry, then cut away tops leaving about a 2-inch (5-cm) stem; or plait together the tops of freshly dug plants. Hang plaits or loose bulbs in nets from the ceiling in a cool, humid, dark place.

HARVESTING A CROP
A 20-foot (6-m) row will yield 5–10 pounds (2.5–5 kg) of garlic. Timing the harvest is a little tricky. Too early and bulbs will be small; too late and the outer skin may tear, making the bulbs store poorly. Wait until leaves begin to turn brown, then check the status of one head before you harvest the crop.

GERANIUM, SCENTED
Pelargonium spp. Geraniaceae

Add the fragrant leaves of rose-scented geraniums to potpourri. The many cultivars offer a variety of flavors, colors and scents. Plant geraniums around roses for a pretty (and pest-controlling) combination.

Best climate and site Zones 9–10 or cool greenhouse in cooler areas.

Ideal soil conditions Can be stood in pots or planted outside in summer.

Growing guidelines Cuttings root quickly and easily from new growth in spring or late summer. Scented geranium grows well in pots near a sunny window. Apply a liquid plant food but hold back on the nitrogen for the best fragrance. Plants more than a year old tend to get over-large. To reclaim an old plant, cut the stems back to short stubs; this will encourage vigorous new growth.

ATTRACTIVE HIDING PLACE
The dense, leafy growth of geraniums provides color, scent and welcome hiding places for insect predators—especially spiders.

ELEGANT FRAGRANCE
The essential oil in geranium leaves has the same constituents as are present in rose oil, which is why geranium fragrance resembles that of rose with a musty, minty-green undertone.

Growing habit Height up to about 3 feet (90 cm), foliage and growth habit vary with species or cultivar; leaves frilly, variegated, ruffled, velvety or smooth.

Flowering time Three to six months from rooting; sometimes inconspicuous.

Pest and disease prevention Vacuum whiteflies from foliage, or control with weekly sprays of insecticidal soap or a botanical insecticide. Garlic sprays may help repel pests. You can purchase parasitic wasps from suppliers of biological controls to control whiteflies indoors. Avoid over-watering so that you don't cause root rot.

Harvesting and storing Pick leaves throughout the summer and dry them, storing in an airtight container, to use in winter potpourris. Use fresh leaves in jellies, or as an aromatic garnish.

Special tips The showy flowering types of geranium are reputed to repel cabbageworms, corn earworms and Japanese beetles. The scented ones are thought to deter red spider mites and cotton aphids. Some gardeners believe that the white-flowered geraniums are effective as a trap crop for Japanese beetles; handpick the beetles from the leaves or destroy the plants.

Keep a pot of scented geraniums near walkways; passersby will brush against the foliage and release the fragrance.

GERMANDER
Teucrium chamaedrys Labiatae

Germander is grown for its boxy ornamental shape, and is well suited to the formal herb garden. The foliage is lightly aromatic and has been traditionally used as a cure for gout, rheumatism and other ailments.

Best climate and site Zones 6–9. Full sun to partial shade.

Ideal soil conditions Well-drained garden soil.

Growing guidelines Best propagated by cuttings, layering or division because seed-raised plants are slow to mature. Plant about 1 foot (30 cm) apart; does well in pots. Can be pruned and trained like a dwarf hedge in knot gardens. Not fully hardy in severe winters. Plant outdoors in the fall.

Growing habit Perennial; height to 2 feet (60 cm) in the temperate midwest; leaves short, broad, oval-shaped and hairy; the square, hairy stalks are of a dirty green color and very weak. Variegated germander is a sort of a common germander with irregular, clear gold splotches on dark green leaves; great for edging a perennial border; winter-hardy into Zone 5 at least; rose-purple flowers; it makes an attractive, long-lived pot plant; can be planted outdoors in the fall. Creeping germander is a close relative that provides a creeping groundcover; it has dark green leaves, dense foliage and rose flowers great for edging a perennial border; winter-hardy into Zone 5 at least; can be planted outdoors in the fall.

Flowering time July to September; small purple to purple-red on leafy spikes; fruit egg-shaped nutlets.

Pest and disease prevention Usually free from pests and diseases; check occasionally.

Harvesting and storing Harvest the leaves during spring and early summer. Dry and store them in an airtight container.

Special tips The whole plant is bitter and slightly aromatic. The fresh leaves, when rubbed, have a penetrating odor, like garlic, and it is said that when cows eat it, their milk is flavored with garlic. It is thought by herbalists that stomachaches can be helped with an infusion prepared from leaves and flower heads. It may also be useful in the treatment of jaundice and liver bile disorders. Its medicinal properties can be attributed to its high content of essential oils, tannin, balsamic and other aromatic compounds.

Other common names Poor man's box, common germander; wall germander.

EASY TO HANDLE

Germander is a pleasure for the novice gardener. It blooms almost constantly and tolerates poor, rocky soil so it can be grown in rock gardens, as a shrub for a low hedge and in the herb garden as well as being a good topiary subject.

GINGER

Zingiber officinale Zingiberaceae

Fresh ginger has a zing that the powdered spice lacks. Grow your own in pots placed outdoors during the warm season. It has the double advantage of being both spicy and kind to your digestive system.

Best climate and site Zone 10 or warm greenhouse. Partial shade.

Ideal soil conditions Fertile, moist, well-drained garden soil.

Growing guidelines Plant rhizomes in pots in a mix containing peat, sand and compost; keep indoors or in a greenhouse in winter, moving the pots outdoors in warm summers. (Thrives in low ground in the tropics and subtropics.)

Growing habit Tender perennial; height 2–4 feet (60–120 cm); leaves strap-shaped, 6–12 inches (15–30 cm) long.

ACTIVE ROOTS

Ginger root has been used for thousands of years, both to spice food and to soothe the digestive system. The action of the root is due to the volatile oil and resin located within the root.

Flowering time Ginger rarely flowers under cultivation; in the wild, it produces dense cone-like spikes on a stalk have yellow-green and purple flowers.

Pest and disease prevention Usually free from pests and diseases. For healthy growth, keep the soil around it moist during the hot summer months.

Harvesting and storing Dig the plant up after one year and remove the leaf stems, cutting away as much root as you need; replant the remaining root. Refrigerate harvested roots wrapped in paper toweling inside a plastic bag, for up to one month. Or dry shaved bits of root and store in an airtight container.

Special tips When using dried ginger in cooking, bruise it well before grinding or grating to

OLD REMEDIES AND RECIPES
Fresh and dried, powdered ginger root has been used for thousands of years to alleviate nausea and improve circulation. Although gingerbread may seem like a recent invention, it was actually being made by Greek bakers more than 4,000 years ago.

release the full flavor. Ginger becomes hotter as it is cooked. Ground ginger loses its aromatic principles quickly, so it is always best to use fresh ground ginger whenever possible. A ginger bath is soothing after exercise; boil a small piece of fresh ginger (or use 3 teaspoons of powdered ginger) and simmer until the water turns yellow. Strain and add to your bath.

Precautions Ginger taken internally is relatively safe, though in extremely large doses, it has the potential to cause depression of the central nervous system and cardiac arrhythmias.

GOLDENROD

Solidago spp. Compositae

Use the dried flowers for flower arrangements or to make a yellow dye. It offers attractive shelter to praying mantids and other predatory insects; in winter, you'll see the egg cases on old stems.

Goldenrod has numerous small, yellow flowers.

Best climate and site Zones 5–9. Thrives in full sun and/or partial shade.

Ideal soil conditions Average to poor, well-drained garden soil.

Growing guidelines Easily grown from seed sown in early spring, or purchase plants from nurseries. Divide mature plants in spring or fall. Can become weedy if the soil is too rich.

Growing habit Height 3–7 feet (90–210 cm); unbranched perennial with simple leaves.

Flowering time August to September; yellow blossoms the second year.

Pest and disease prevention Usually free from pests and diseases.

Harvesting and storing The leaves and tops are used; they should be collected during the flowering period and dried in bunches or on screens; quickly turns black without adequate air circulation. Store in airtight containers. Use the leaves to make a tea to treat flatulence.

Special tips Plant in masses or weave clumps into ornamental plantings near the vegetable garden to attract beneficials. Many species self-sow freely or spread quickly by creeping roots, so don't plant them in the vegetable patch. Plumes of goldenrod and purple asters are the perfect combination for fall, in fields or in a border. Goldenrod may inhibit the growth of sugar maple and black locust by releasing an allelopathic substance. They are often blamed for causing drippy noses and itchy, watering eyes in the fall, but the real culprit is an inconspicuous weed called ragweed, which produces allergy-causing pollen grains.

POLLEN RICH

Goldenrod is one of the best plants for attracting beneficials to the garden. Its fall-blooming plumes or spikes are tightly clustered with thousands of tiny flowers rich with pollen and nectar.

HOP

Humulus lupulus Cannabaceae

Hop is an attractive vining perennial for arbors and screens, as well as an essential ingredient in bitter beer. Oil of hops is used in perfumes and the stem is used for industrial fiber.

Best climate and site Zones 6–9; will stand temperatures as low as −35°F (−37°C). Full sun.

Ideal soil conditions Moist and rich soil.

Growing guidelines Take basal cuttings in spring and grow singly in pots for one year before planting out, then plant in clumps of three to five plants spaced about 6 inches (15 cm) apart. Place poles for the twining stems at the base of plants before growth begins. In the fall, remove both poles and old growth. Mulch with compost each spring. Seeds are slow to germinate and grow, so are not good for propagation.

CALMING EFFECT
Hop pickers used to tire easily, gaining hops a reputation as a safe sedative. Later, pillows filled with hops were used for insomnia.

Growing habit Height 20–30 feet (6–9 m) in one season; prickly, rough climbing stems with dark green, lobed, grapelike leaves.

Flowering time Mid- to late summer; bears male and female flowers on separate plants in the third year; female flowers resemble papery cones.

Pest and disease prevention Usually disease- and pest-free.

Harvesting and storing Collect female cones in late summer when mature and immediately dry them in an oven at 125–150°F (50–65°C). Does not store well, so use promptly.

FEMALE SOCIETY
The hop is dioecious, meaning that male and female flowers are on separate plants. Only the ripened cones of the female hop plant are used in brewing.

HOREHOUND
Marrubium vulgare Labiatae

Plant horehound to attract bees to your garden.
The menthol-flavored leaves are said to soothe
coughs when taken as a syrup or decoction. It
flourishes in waste places and by roadsides.

Best climate and site Zones
6–9. Full sun to partial shade.

Ideal soil conditions Average,
well-drained garden soil.

Growing guidelines Sow seed
about ⅛ inch (3 mm) deep in early
spring, thinning to 10–20 inches
(25–50 cm). Horehound
germinates slowly, then grows
easily. Divide mature plants in
spring. Plant in a well-drained
location, since horehound will
die in winter in wet soil.

Growing habit Perennial;
height 2–3 feet (60–90 cm);
branching, square stems with
round, woolly leaves.

FULL FOLIAGE
The leaf surfaces of horehound are
dotted with small glands that contain
an aromatic oil. The leaves also contain
lignin, tannin and resins.

Flowering time June to September; first blooms are fairly insignificant white flowers arranged in rings around the upper part of the stems; small white tubular blooms in dense whorls are produced in the upper leaf axils in the second year. The flowers die off, leaving a spiny burr containing four small brown or black seeds.

Pest and disease prevention Usually free from pests and diseases.

Harvesting and storing The first year, cut foliage sparingly. The second year, harvest leaves when flower buds appear, chop and dry them, then store in airtight containers. Horehound extract can be distilled from the dried leaves and flowers of the plant, and used as a tea for soothing sore throats, colds and coughs. It is also brewed and made into horehound ale. Candied horehound is best made from the fresh plant by boiling it down until the juice is extracted, then adding sugar before boiling this again, until it has become thick enough to pour into a paper case and be cut into squares when cool.

Special tips Grown in pastures with livestock, horehound can cause problems because it is very bitter. Grazing animals tend to concentrate on other plants in the paddock, which cuts down the competition with horehound and leaves it to spread. However, if animals are forced to eat it, their meat and milk have a strong offensive smell and flavor. The most significant negative effect of the weed is that the burrs attach themselves easily to wool and are difficult to remove, so the sale price of the wool will be downgraded. Because the plant is drought-tolerant, it can use the occasional drought to suddenly increase its range.

Other common names White horehound, hoarhound, bull's blood, horus, marvel, white hoarhound.

Horehound leaves make a soothing drink.

HORSERADISH
Armoracia rusticana Cruciferae

Horseradish is the root of a deep-rooted perennial. Folklore claims that horseradish should be planted near potatoes to protect them from disease. This ancient herb (one of the five bitter herbs of the Jewish Passover festival) is a native of eastern Europe, but now grows in other parts of Europe as well as the United States.

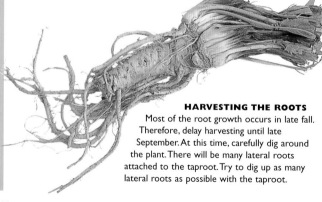

HARVESTING THE ROOTS
Most of the root growth occurs in late fall. Therefore, delay harvesting until late September. At this time, carefully dig around the plant. There will be many lateral roots attached to the taproot. Try to dig up as many lateral roots as possible with the taproot.

Best climate and site Zones 6–9. Full sun.

Ideal soil conditions Fertile, moist but well-drained soil.

Growing guidelines Plant when the straight, young roots are about 9 inches (23 cm) long and ½ inch (1 cm) wide so that the crown or growing point is 2–5 inches (5–7.5 cm) below the soil surface, and plants are 12–18 inches (30–45 cm) apart.

Growing habit Second-year plants grow 2 feet (60 cm) tall; leaves are stalked and oblong.

Flowering time Early summer; small, white blossoms do not produce viable seed.

Pest and disease prevention Usually free from pests and diseases; check occasionally.

Harvesting and storing

Though it has spiky green leaves that can be used in salads, horseradish is grown mainly for its large, white, pungently spicy roots. Harvest roots in fall and winter and scrub them before storing in the refrigerator, or pack in dry sand in the cellar for spring planting. Or leave roots in the soil and harvest as required. Peel before using.

Special tips Harvest early for the most tender roots. If buying fresh horseradish from the market, choose roots that are firm with no sign of blemishes or withering.

HEADY GROWTH

Horseradish is one of the more aromatic herbs. A small patch is more than sufficient to meet family needs, for it can easily overtake the garden plot. A thorough, deep cultivation will help to control its spread.

Plant by Plant Guide

HORSETAIL
Equisetum spp. Equisetaceae

A primitive, spore-bearing, grasslike plant
containing silica, horsetail has often been used as
a pot-scrubber and for sanding wood. Look for it
along low-lying edges of woods.

Best climate and site Zones 5–9. Full sun to partial shade.

Ideal soil conditions Humusy, moist soil.

Growing guidelines Rarely cultivated, since it is difficult to eradicate once established. Plant in buckets to prevent its spread. Propagate in the fall by dividing mature plants.

Growing habit Perennial; height 4–18 inches (10–45 cm); primitive spore-bearing herb, with hollow stems impregnated with silica; occurs on all landmasses except Australia. From rhizomes or

HARDY HERB
Horsetail can survive and even flourish in soils severely contaminated by chemical pollutants. It must have wet areas to become established, but once in place it can tolerate very dry conditions.

roots, it sends up both a green stalk and a flesh-colored, leafless stalk crowned with a spore-producing strobilus, or cone; a few species produce a single green stalk with terminal cones.

Flowering time April; spikes form atop stalks, and soft terminal cone-like structures release spores.

Pest and disease prevention Usually free from pests and diseases; check occasionally.

Harvesting and storing Cut stems just above the root, dry in the sun and tie in bundles.

Special tips Dried stems are said to act as a garden fungicide; steep the stems in hot water, strain, and spray on plants outdoors.

Precautions Horsetail is toxic when large doses are taken internally.

Other common names Bottle brush, scouring brush.

NATURAL REPAIRS
The stems contain large amounts of silica, which is used by the body in the production and repair of connective tissues and accelerates the healing of broken bones. Our bodies also use silica to maintain and repair the nails, hair, skin, eyes and cell walls.

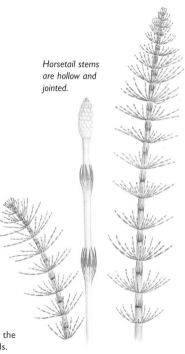

Horsetail stems are hollow and jointed.

HYSSOP

Hyssopus officinalis Labiatae

The blossoms of this evergreen, shrubby plant attract honeybees and other beneficials. The leaves add a minty aroma and flavor to salads and soups. Oil of hyssop is used in liqueurs and perfumes.

Best climate and site Zones 6–9. Prefers full sun.

Ideal soil conditions Light, well-drained soil.

Growing guidelines Sow seed about ¼ inch (5 mm) deep in early spring, thinning to 1 foot (30 cm). Take cuttings or divide mature plants in spring or fall. Prune to 6 inches (15 cm) in spring and lightly mulch with compost. Replace every four to five years.

Growing habit Height 1–2 feet (30–60 cm).

Flowering time June to August; blue or violet, in whorls along the stem tops.

Pest and disease prevention Usually disease- and pest-free.

Harvesting and storing For medicinal use, harvest only green material. Cut stems just before flowers open and hang bunches to dry; store in an airtight container.

Special tips A hot tea of the leaves and flowers or just the flowers can be taken at the early

Only the green material is used medicinally.

stages of colds and flu to promote sweating, or any time there is chest congestion or coughing to promote expectoration. A cooled tea can be use externally as a compress on scalds, minor burns and bruises. The tincture (alcoholic extract) can be used in combination with other expectorant herbs like elecampane, licorice and anise for bronchitis and congestion. The essential oil of hyssop is pleasant-smelling and can be used as a chest rub when mixed with a carrier oil.

Caution High doses of the essential oil may cause convulsions. Always use diluted, and only as recommended.

WORTHY HERB
Hyssop is an herb well worth growing in the garden. It is both ornamental and functional, and a great bee plant. As a natural expectorant, it has many uses during the winter and spring months.

LAVENDER, ENGLISH

Lavandula angustifolia Labiatae

Most herb growers never have enough lavender since this aromatic garden ornamental is also useful for crafts and cosmetics. The silvery foliage and purple blossoms are stunning in borders, and attract bees.

Pot French lavender for use on sunny decks and patios.

Best climate and site Zones 6–9. Full sun to light shade.

Ideal soil conditions Light, well-drained, ideally limey soil. Neutral or slightly alkaline is best.

HERBAL HEALING
Lavender oil is used in many commercially prepared products for its antiseptic and soothing properties. Dried lavender flowers have a long-lasting scent and are often used in potpourris.

Growing guidelines As seeds do not always produce plants identical to the original, the best way to propagate is by cuttings 2–3 inches (5–7 cm) long, taken from sideshoots in spring or fall; space 12–30 inches (30–75 cm) apart. Place cuttings in a well-drained medium; transplant them as soon as they root to avoid rot. Pinch away flowers on first-year plants to encourage vigorous growth. Provide shelter from winter winds; in areas with cold, wet winters, loose, well-drained soil is the secret to success. Some growers find that plants weaken with age, requiring replacement every five years. Remove old plants each spring, and lightly mulch with compost or well-aged manure before planting new, young plants. The hardiness of lavender varies with each species, but generally it's extremely drought-tolerant. Let the soil dry well between waterings. Excess fertility will make the silver-gray foliage fade to green.

Growing habit Shrub; height 2–3 feet (60–90 cm); shrubby with slender gray-green leaves.

Flowering time June to July; lavender-blue blossoms on tall, straight spikes.

AN ORNAMENTAL REPELLENT
As well as looking wonderful, big bushes of lavender in your garden may act as a fly and tick repellent.

Pest and disease prevention
Generally trouble-free.

Harvesting and storing For the most intense scent in fresh and dried arrangements, gather the flower stems just as the flowers are opening, preferably in dry weather. The leaves, which are bitter and sometimes used in European cooking, can be harvested after the first year of growth and then picked at any time. Hang bunches of lavender upside down, away from sunlight, to dry. When using the dried flowers in potpourris or herbal sachets, keep the stems; they can be burned, like incense, or in a log fire to scent the smoke.

NATIONALITY TRAITS
French lavender has attractive, fernlike leaves. It's less hardy than English lavender.

Special tips Plant lavender as a hedge or border or to configure knot gardens. In borders combine them with other plants that need excellent drainage such as yarrows and sundrops. Incorporate it into vegetable and ornamental gardens to increase populations of visiting

beneficial insects. Used in a spray, lavender is reputed to control pests of cotton. It has also shown some repellent effect toward clothes moths; dry a sprig and slip it in a pocket or pin it to a sleeve in sweater drawers or closets. Oil of lavender is said to rejuvenate the skin of face and hands so that they look younger. At the least, it'll make you smell good!

Cultivars ❖ 'Dwarf Blue' has dark blue flowers on 1-foot (30-cm) plants.
❖ 'Hidcote' grows to 2 feet (60 cm) tall with purple-blue flowers.

MORE AND LESS
Italian lavender produces more oil of a lesser quality than English lavender. Its oil is used to perfume cheap goods or sometimes mixed with higher-quality oil to add bulk. The oil is distilled from the glands tucked around tiny hairs on the flowers, leaves and stems.

Gather lavender into neat bunches for a bouquet.

❖ 'Jean Davis' has pale pink flowers.
❖ 'Munstead' has lavender-blue flowers on 2-foot (60-cm) plants.

Other species ❖ French lavender (*L. stoechas*): Half-hardy with purple flowers and gray-green leaves.
❖ Italian lavender (*L. latifolia*): Also called spike lavender.

LEMON BALM

Melissa officinalis Labiatae

The leaves of lemon balm are strongly lemon-scented. The dainty white flowers attract many honeybees.

Use dried lemon balm leaves in sachets.

Best climate and site Zones 6–9. Full sun to partial shade.

Ideal soil conditions Any well-drained soil.

Growing guidelines Sow shallowly in spring, thinning to 18–24 inches (45–60 cm); readily self-sows. Take cuttings or divide older plants in spring or fall. Each fall, cut away old stalks.

Growing habit Perennial; height 1–2 feet (30–60 cm); stems square, branching, with oval, toothed leaves.

Flowering time June to October; small white tubular blossoms in bunches in the upper leaf axils.

MULCH FOR HEALTH
Keep the soil around lemon balm moist, and the weeds away, with a layer of organic mulch.

Pest and disease prevention
Thin dense plantings for best
air circulation, to prevent
powdery mildew. Rarely bothered
by insects.

Harvesting and storing
Collect leaves in late summer and
dry quickly to prevent them from
turning black. Cut the entire plant,
leaving about 2 inches (5 cm) of
stem. Use leaves fresh in salads
and for cooking, or dry them for
making tea.

Special tips The leaves lowest
on the plant are said to be highest
in essential oils.

Other common names Sweet
balm, bee balm.

STRONG SCENT
The bold lemony fragrance given off
by volatile essential oils in lemon balm
can make pests flee.

LEMONGRASS

Cymbopogon citratus Graminae

The slim, grassy foliage of lemongrass provides a contrast with broad-leaved garden herbs. Use the white, thick base of the leaves in cooking. The dried foliage is tasty in tea.

Best climate and site Zones 9–10 or greenhouse; can be placed outside in pots or planted out during the summer in full sun to partial shade.

Ideal soil conditions Well-drained garden soil enriched with organic matter.

Growing guidelines Propagate by division of older plants. Trim the leaves to several inches before dividing.

Growing habit Tender perennial; height 6 feet (1.8 m); forms dense clumps of typical grass leaves.

Flowering time Seldom flowers.

MEDICINAL VALUES
The essential oil distilled from lemongrass, and the dried foliage, are used to soothe fevers and in treatments for respiratory problems, sore throats and oily skin.

Pest and disease prevention
Usually free from pests and diseases.

Harvesting and storing Snip fresh foliage as needed anytime in summer. Use the white stem base in cooking.

Special tips Lemongrass oil blends well with the oils of basil, geranium, jasmine and lavender; use in oil burners and mixed into a base oil for massage. Sprigs of fresh lemongrass are often used in recipes with coconut milk.

Other common names
Oilgrass, fevergrass, West Indian lemon.

NATURAL SELECTION
Individual leaves of a lemongrass plant regularly die off; this doesn't indicate a problem with the plant and there is no need to remove the dead foliage.

LEMON VERBENA
Aloysia triphylla Verbenaceae

Though it is not hardy, the strong lemon aroma and flavor of lemon verbena is worth the extra care required; it is wonderful in cosmetics and teas. Dried, it retains its scent for over two years.

Best climate and site Zones 9–10 or south-facing walls outside for 8; frost-free greenhouse in cooler areas.

Ideal soil conditions Fertile, light, well-drained soil; preferably alkaline.

Growing guidelines In cold climates, grow in pots placed outdoors in summer and indoors in winter (though plants that have been grown in poor soil, and thrived, may survive cold winters). Keep the soil moist but never soggy; feed with compost water regularly. Pinch tips to encourage bushy growth. In the fall, prune away long branches before bringing pots indoors. If the plants are to be

CHANGING COLORS
The stem of lemon verbena is ridged and green when the plant is young, and woody and red in later years.

The oil is used in cosmetics for the hair and face.

overwintered in a greenhouse, keep the temperature at 45°F (7°C).

Growing habit Height 5–10 feet (1.5–3 m); tender, deciduous, woody shrub with light green lance-like leaves in whorls.

Flowering time Late summer to fall; tiny white to lavender blossoms in terminal panicles.

Pest and disease prevention Wash mites from foliage with a spray of water directed at the undersides of leaves. For stubborn infestations, wipe infected areas with cotton soaked in alcohol, or spray with a botanical insecticide, like citrus oil, pyrethrin or rotenone.

Harvesting and storing Snip sprigs of leaves or cut foliage back halfway in midsummer and again in the fall. Dry foliage in a shady spot; store in an airtight container.

Special tips Will train as a mop-headed standard.

SPECIAL SCENT
Lemon verbena has a special place in a garden that has been designed for its fragrances or for a fragrant section of your yard. The sharp, lemony scent of its foliage is well complemented by bergamot, lavender, sweet woodruff and clove pink. Like all herbs, its scent is strongest on contact.

LOVAGE

Levisticum officinale Umbelliferae

If you are unsuccessful growing celery, try this easy and flavorful substitute. Some companion gardeners claim that lovage improves the growth and flavor of vegetable crops.

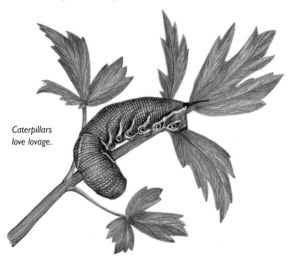

Caterpillars love lovage.

Best climate and site Zones 6–9. Prefers full sun but tolerates partial shade.

Ideal soil conditions Fertile, moist, but well-drained soil.

Growing guidelines Sow ripe seed shallowly in fall; thin to 3 feet (90 cm) apart. Plant lovage seedlings 3 feet (90 cm) apart in spring, as soon as the soil is thawed and dry enough to work in; it is one of the hardiest of the cool-weather plants. Prune away flowers to encourage vegetative growth. Each spring, mulch with compost or well-rotted manure. Replace plants every four to five years.

Growing habit Perennial; height to 6 feet (1.8 m) or more in optimum conditions; hollow, ribbed stems; glossy leaves.

Flowering time June to July; tiny greenish yellow flowers in umbels.

Pest and disease prevention Mainly trouble-free. Occasionally it may be attacked by caterpillars; remove and destroy any found.

Harvesting and storing Once established, harvest leaves as needed for fresh use. In fall, bunch foliage and stems and hang to dry. Or blanch small bunches before freezing for winter use. Seeds are ripe and ready to harvest when the fruits begin to split open. Dig roots in late fall, wash and slice into ½-inch (1-cm) pieces, and dry before storing.

Special tips The leaves, stems, and seeds all have a savory celery-like flavor. Try the chopped leaves in potato salad and cream soups.

LURING LOVAGE

Lovage is recommended as a trap crop to lure tomato hornworms away from tomatoes; handpick the pests or cut off and destroy infested foliage. The umbels of tiny greenish yellow flowers attract parasitic and predaceous insects to the garden, and the bushy plants provide shelter for predatory insects. A single plant may be all you need as a trap crop. Plant it at the back of the ornamental border for an eye-catching accent.

MADDER, DYER'S

Rubia tinctorum Rubiaceae

The foliage and root of madder are used to produce brown, orange, pink and red dyes. Madder needs space to sprawl, but will climb if planted beside a wooden fence.

Best climate and site Zones 6–9. Thrives in full sun and will tolerate light shade.

Ideal soil conditions Fertile, well-drained soil; preferably a neutral pH.

Growing guidelines If planting from seed, sow shallowly indoors in spring and set out in late spring or early fall, 1 foot (30 cm) apart. Once established, new plants will spring up from roots.

Growing habit Perennial; height up to 4 feet (1.2 m); reddish brown, succulent root; with prickly, weak, four-sided stems with joints. (The stems are so slender that they can't support the weight of the plant when it climbs. The prickles help the plant cling to the surface it is climbing. When the plant is not climbing, the stems lie along the ground.) Madder has large, lance-shaped, rough-edged leaves.

Flowering time Early summer to late fall; loose spikes of small, yellow, starry flowers in second or third year. Followed by small, round, red to black fruit.

Pest and disease prevention Usually free from pests and diseases; check occasionally.

Harvesting and storing Dig the roots of the plants after about three years, and after their flowering season in fall; use the roots fresh or dry to make dyes for cloth or leather.

Special tips The depth of color you can achieve when making a dye from the madder root depends on the mordant, or fixative, you use and the immersion time. A mordant of alum and cream of tartar will produce a rose-red; chrome will produce a garnet, orange or rust color; tin will yield a bright red. To make a dye bath using madder, chop the same amount of root as the weight of the cloth or wool you are going to dye. Place it in a muslin bag and soak it in 5 gallons (22.5 L) of tepid water overnight. The next day, simmer it for about three hours, or until the water turns the color you want. Remove the root material, cool the liquid a little and add the cloth. Return to a simmer for about two hours. Leave to cool and then remove the cloth. Rinse it in warm water, then tepid water and then in cold water. Madder root is also used medicinally as a diuretic, for urinary disorders and to prevent kidney stones. Only use powdered root purchased from a reputable herbalist. A tea from the leaves may relieve constipation; use the prickly leaves in facial scrubs.

FOOD COLORING

Madder is sometimes used as animal fodder. Because of the coloring properties of the madder root, the milk, urine and bones of animals that eat the plant are colored shades of red through to brown.

Marjoram, Sweet

Origanum majorana Labiatae

Sweet marjoram is a bushy, aromatic plant with a mild oregano taste. In summer, the plentiful clusters of tiny flowers attract many beneficial insects to the garden.

Best climate and site Zones 6–9. Full sun.

Ideal soil conditions Light, well-drained soil.

Growing guidelines The seeds are small and slow to germinate; if you want to try growing plants this way, sow seed shallowly indoors in spring; it germinates slowly. You can also buy plants at a garden center. Set out after danger of frost, spacing clumps of several plants 6–12 inches (15–30 cm) apart. Cut back by half just before blooming, to maintain vegetative growth. In the fall divide roots

SPRAWLING HABIT

Sweet marjoram can sprawl to cover a good-sized piece of ground; you'll need to either prune it back or give it plenty of room.

An oil extracted from marjoram flowers is helpful in treating sunburn and acne.

and bring indoors in pots or place in a frost-free greenhouse.

Growing habit Height to 2 feet (60 cm); bushy, tender perennial. The stems are square and covered with fine hairs. It has a dense, shallow root system

Flowering time August to September; white or pink blossoms. The flowers have knot-like shapes before blossoming.

Pest and disease prevention Usually free from pests and diseases.

Harvesting and storing Cut fresh leaves as needed for cooking; hang small bunches to dry, then store in airtight containers.

Special tips Dried marjoram retains its flavor all winter. The fresh leaves can be used as a substitute for oregano in pizza, pasta dishes and recipes that use eggplant. Its delicate flavor is also good in egg and potato dishes. The cuisines of Italy, France and Portugal use marjoram extensively. Some companion gardeners recommend planting sweet marjoram to improve the growth and flavor of other nearby herbs. Plant it with sage, chives and other herbs, or add it to the flower garden.

Other common names Knotted marjoram.

PRETTY IN POTS
Marjoram grows well in a container and is a pretty addition to a patio or deck; in summer, the bushy plant is dotted with appealing clusters of tiny purple and pink flowers.

MARSH MALLOW

Althaea officinalis Malvaceae

The roots of marsh mallow were originally used to produce the consistency typical of the confection marshmallow. Now the plant is grown for its medicinal and culinary uses.

Best climate and site Zones 6–9. Full sun.

Ideal soil conditions Light soil that stays damp.

Growing guidelines Sow seed shallowly outdoors in spring, thinning to 2 feet (60 cm); divide clumps or take basal cuttings from foliage or roots in the fall.

Growing habit Height to about 4 feet (1.2 m) but often less; perennial roots; soft, gray, velvety foliage dies down in fall.

MELLOW MALLOW
Marsh mallow is used in treatments for skin inflammations and to cleanse and soothe dry skin.

Flowering time August to September; pink or bluish-white mallow-like blossoms followed by circular, downy seedpods called "cheeses;" each carpel holds one seed.

Pest and disease prevention Usually free from pests and diseases; remove problem plants.

Harvesting and storing Harvest the leaves in fall just before flowering. Collect and dry flowers at their peak. If you plan to use the roots, dig them in fall from plants that are at least two years old; slice the root before drying.

Special tips Use the leaves to add a fresh flavor to salads; make an infusion with the leaves or the flowers to use as a gargle for sore throats, and as a drink for soothing bronchial and gastric problems. The sweet-tasting, sticky root can be scrubbed and cooked like potatoes. The fresh root can also be grated and used in a poultice or ointment for the treatment of all kinds of skin problems; a powder of the dried root can be applied as a face scrub.

Other common names White mallow, sweet weed, mallards, mauls, schloss tea, mortification root, althea, wymote.

WILD GROWTH
Marsh mallow is often found growing wild in fields and woodlands and is easily identified by its large flowers and grayish-green, lobed leaves. This very hardy herb especially likes moist places, such as salt marshes and land that drains to rivers or oceans.

MINT
Mentha spp. Labiatae

The mints are herbaceous perennials that thrive in most locations. The fresh and dried foliage provide flavoring for both sweet and savory dishes. The flowers attract many beneficial insects.

Best climate and site Zones 5–9. Full sun or partial shade.

Ideal soil conditions Moist, well-drained soil.

Growing guidelines Propagate from new plants that spring up along roots, or by cuttings in spring or fall. Allow 12–18 inches (30–45 cm) between plants. Mint is a rampant spreader. To control, plant in bottomless cans 10 inches (25 cm) deep, or in large pots. Top-dress with compost or well-rotted manure in fall.

MINT ON THE MOVE
Mint is notoriously invasive, so don't allow it free rein in your garden. If you want to grow mint around your crops, plant it in pots and set the pots near the plants you want to protect. Place a saucer beneath the pot to prevent the roots from creeping into the soil.

Growing habit Height up to 30 inches (75 cm) or more; square stems with lance-like leaves.

Flowering time July to August; tiny purple or pink blossoms in whorled spikes.

Pest and disease prevention Usually free from pests and diseases; check occasionally.

Harvesting and storing Harvest fresh leaves as needed. Just before blooming, cut the stalks and hang in bunches to dry; store in airtight containers.

USEFUL SCENT
These strong-smelling plants are favorites with companion gardeners who believe that the sharp fragrance repels insect pests. Some believe that mint also improves the vigor and flavor of cabbage and tomatoes.

Special tips Mints are said to do well when planted where water drips, such as near outdoor taps that are used often in summer. Mint oil has many medicinal uses and may have fungicidal or pest-repellent uses; try a homemade spray using the fresh leaves. Any of the mints make a refreshing addition to ice-cold water in summer and chewing on the leaves will relieve bad breath or a foul taste in the mouth.

Species ❖ Apple mint (*M. suaveolens*): Apple-scented, has broader, and hairy leaves; a variegated cultivar is sometimes called pineapple mint.
❖ Corsican mint (*M. requienii*):

MINT COLOGNE

Eau-de-cologne mint has the sweetest smelling scent and is the mint most often used in perfumes and soaps. This mint also makes a pleasant, citrusy tea.

Creeping growth habit, good as a groundcover but less hardy than most mints; tiny, bright green leaves with a strong peppermint flavor; also called crème-de-menthe plant.

❖ Eau-de-cologne mint (*M.* x *piperita* var. *citrata*): Crushed leaves give off lemony aroma; also called bergamot mint.

❖ Japanese mint (*M. arvensis* var. *piperescens*): Large, green leaves with hairy stems and strong peppermint flavor; major source of menthol in Japan.

❖ Peppermint (*M.* x *piperita*): Leaves smooth, lance-like; smooth, purple stems; height 2–4 feet (60–120 cm); strong peppermint flavor; rampant grower; likes lots of water; rarely bears fertile seeds; must be started by cuttings or division.

❖ Spearmint (*M. spicata*): Lance-shaped, serrated leaves with spearmint flavor.

Basil mint

Common mint

PEPPERMINT PREPARATIONS

Peppermint oil and peppermint tea are used to relieve colds, insomnia, headaches and abdominal pains. A few drops of oil in a bath may also relieve itchy skin and can be added to a massage oil for application on bruises and sprains.

MUSTARD

Brassica spp. Cruciferae

Most mustards are annuals or biennials. Some are "winter annuals" that remain green even when buried in snow. The cultivated species can benefit many kinds of crops by deterring pests.

Best climate and site Zones 6–10. Full sun.

Ideal soil conditions Ordinary well-drained soil.

Growing guidelines Easily grows from seed sown shallowly outdoors from early spring until fall; thin to 9 inches (23 cm). Mustard can self-sow if allowed to. Prepare beds with compost or well-rotted manure, but avoid excessive applications of manure, as this could damage the roots.

TROUBLE IN THE WILD

Unlike its cultivated relative, wild mustard may bring more troubles to the garden than it prevents. It hosts insect pests, such as pea aphids, and may attract cutworms and other pests which will then move on to cabbage and other garden crops. Chemicals released by wild mustard may stunt the growth of lettuce.

Growing habit Very hardy; height 4–6 feet (1.2–1.8 m); leaves various shapes.

Flowering time Early summer; four-petaled yellow flowers in terminal racemes.

Pest and disease prevention Can attract the same pests as its close relatives in the cabbage family, but usually trouble-free.

Harvesting and storing Collect and dry seeds when ripe.

Special tips Brussels sprouts and collards intercropped with wild mustard may have fewer cabbage aphids; collards may have fewer flea beetles. Cultivated and weedy mustard species are reputed to improve the vigor of beans, grapevines and fruit trees.

Species ❖ Black mustard (*B. nigra*): Much-branched annual; height to 6 feet (1.8 m); cultivated as the main source of table mustard.
❖ White mustard (*B. hirta*): Annual; height to 4 feet (1.2 m); cultivated for greens, and mustard- and oil-producing seeds.

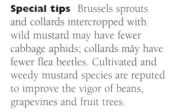

Mustard seeds have a sharp, bitter taste. The black and brown seeds are used in sauces and curries; the white seeds are used in pickles.

HOT MUSTARD
Mustard's tang gets hotter as the air temperatures rise. For the mildest flavor, pick young leaves early in the day. You can start picking eight to ten days after the seeds have been sown.

NASTURTIUM

Tropaeolum majus Tropaeolaceae

Nasturtiums are a favorite of both gardeners and cooks. The blossoms are a reliable source of color all summer long and the spurred flowers attract hummingbirds.

Nasturtiums blossom in a variety of colors.

Best climate and site Zones 6–10. Blooms best in full sun.

Ideal soil conditions Average, moist, well-drained, nutrient-poor soil. Nasturtiums tend to produce more leaves than flowers if you plant them in rich soil.

Growing guidelines Sow seed outdoors ¼–¾ inches (1–2 cm) deep after the last frost, when the soil is warm in spring; thin plants to 6–9 inches (15–23 cm). For bushels of blooms, hold back the nitrogen. Also does well as a potted annual.

Growing habit Annual; height up to 1–2 feet (30–60 cm) tall, or for bush cultivars 6–10 feet (2–3 m) for climbers.

Flowering time Summer; red, orange or yellow funnel-shaped, sweet-smelling blossoms.

Pest and disease prevention
Wash away aphids with a spray of
water. For persistent populations,
spray with insecticidal soap.

Harvesting and storing Snip
young, fresh leaves and blossoms
all summer as needed for salads.
In fall, pickle the unopened buds
for homemade capers.

Special tips Look for dwarf,
vining and variegated types in
seed catalogues.

Other common names
Indian cress.

KEEPING NASTIES AT BAY
Nasturtiums are said to deter pests,
including whiteflies, from beans,
cabbage and its relatives and
cucumbers. Some companion
gardeners plant nasturtiums where
they will later plant their squash,
hoping to keep squash bugs away.

NETTLE, COMMON

Urtica dioica Urticaceae

Though it is a noxious pest to gardeners, nettle is high in vitamin C and is used extensively by practitioners of homeopathic medicine. The fibers can be used to make cloth.

Best climate and site Zones 5–9. Full sun to partial shade.

Ideal soil conditions All garden soils.

Growing guidelines Sow seed shallowly outdoors in early spring; self-sows readily or divide in winter or spring.

Growing habit Rhizomatous perennial; height 2–6 feet (60–180 cm); whole plant has stinging hairs.

Flowering time June to September; greenish male flowers in loose sprays; female flowers more densely clustered together.

NETTLE TEA

Harvest a batch of nettle leaves for a tea that will stimulate digestion and may reduce susceptibility to migraine. The juice is helpful for oily skins.

Pest and disease prevention
Usually free from pests and diseases; check occasionally.

Harvesting and storing
Harvest whole plant above the root, just before flowering; hang in bunches to dry. Cook fresh greens like spinach. Collect seeds and dry on paper. Wear heavy gloves when harvesting.

Precautions When touched, the hairs inject an irritating substance into the skin that will cause it to swell and sting for several hours. Rub dock leaves onto stings to soothe them.

FIELD NETTLE
Nettle is one of the most common wild herbs and is generally considered to be a weed in the home garden. If you would prefer not to grow it but you want to use it medicinally or in cosmetics, you can usually find it growing by the roadside.

OREGANO (MARJORAM)

Origanum vulgare Labiatae

Interplant perennial oregano at permanent spots in the vegetable garden, or use it as a border. Oregano can also be attractive in flower beds. The sprigs, with their small, rounded leaves and miniature blossoms, make an attractive garnish.

POTTED REPELLENT
Like other strongly aromatic herbs, oregano has gained a reputation as a pest repellent. Planted in pots, it can be moved around the garden as needed.

The leaves will retain their flavor when dried.

Best climate and site Zones 6–9. Full sun.

Ideal soil conditions
Well-drained, average garden soil.

Growing guidelines Sow seed shallowly indoors in winter for best germination; sow outdoors if soil temperature is above 45°F (7°C). Plant in clumps 1 foot (30 cm) apart. Prune regularly for best shape. Since seedlings will not always produce the same flavor as the original plants, take cuttings or divide roots in spring or early fall for best results. Lightly mulch each spring with organic matter such as compost or well-rotted manure.

Growing habit Perennial; height 12–30 in (30–75 cm); herbaceous, somewhat woody-based.

Flowering time July to September; tubular, rose-purple, rarely white blossoms in broad terminal clusters.

Pest and disease prevention Usually free from pests and diseases; check occasionally.

Harvesting and storing Snip fresh sprigs as needed all summer; cut whole plant in June and again in late August; hang foliage in bunches to dry.

Other common names Wild marjoram.

TASTELESS VARIETIES
Wild oregano is a sprawler and usually doesn't have much of the signature oregano flavor; it does, however, produce bountiful flowers for dried arrangements. If you're planting oregano for its culinary use, buy the plants to make sure you've got the traditional, sharp-flavored herb.

ORRIS

Iris x germanica var. *florentina* Iridaceae

Orris is the root of the florentine iris. Dried, it has a strong, long-lasting violet fragrance and is commonly used as a fixative for potpourri; it helps to preserve the scents of the dried plant material.

Best climate and site Zones 6–9. Full sun.

Ideal soil conditions Ordinary, well-drained soil.

Growing guidelines Plant after flowering or in early spring, leaving the top surface of the rhizome above the soil. Divide the roots every two to three years (it takes two to three years for the rhizomes to reach maturity) in early fall to promote vigorous flowering. Half the divided root should be left above the soil so that it doesn't rot.

Growing habit Height to 30 inches (75 cm).

Flowering time May to June; blossoms are large, white and tinged with blue or purple.

FRESH SCENT
As well as its extensive use as a fixative in potpourris, dried, powdered orris root is used on its own in sachets; stored in linen and clothes cupboards, it imparts a fresh scent. It can also be used as a dry shampoo.

Pest and disease prevention Usually free from pests and diseases.

Harvesting and storing Harvest orris at maturity. If using the roots for their aroma, dig them up in fall (don't worry that the fresh root has very little scent). Wash and split them, then cut them into small pieces before drying the pieces on paper or on a screen. Grind them to a powder in an old blender, or use the fine mesh of a food grater (it's easier to do it while the pieces are still slightly moist). Store the powder in a dark, glass container for at least two years; the violet fragrance needs this time to mature.

Special tips Use one tablespoon of orris fixative for each quart (1 L) of dried base. Orris used to be used medicinally for coughs, colic and bad breath, but it is now thought to be too powerful a purgative and generally dangerous when taken internally.

IRIS WITHOUT THE ORRIS
Even if you have no use for orris, the florentine iris is an attractive plant with slender, sword-shaped leaves and, in summer, magnificent flowers. It blooms in a wide variety of colors.

PARSLEY, CURLED
Petroselinum crispum var. *crispum* Umbelliferae

Parsley is required in so many recipes that it is a feature of most herb gardens. The delicate, dark green foliage makes it an excellent plant for borders or growing on window sills.

Best climate and site Zones 5–9. Full sun to partial shade.

Ideal soil conditions
Moderately rich, well-drained soil.

Growing guidelines Sow parsley seed shallowly outdoors in early spring when soil reaches 50°F (10°C), thinning to 8 inches (20 cm) apart; it's notoriously slow to germinate. Alternatively, soak seeds overnight in warm water before sowing in peat pots indoors in early spring. Remove all flower stalks that form, and prune away

HELPING OTHERS

Asparagus, roses and tomatoes are all said to benefit from nearby parsley plantings. Many companion gardeners are convinced that parsley repels asparagus beetles. Others believe that parsley reduces carrot rust flies and beetles on roses. Interplanted parsley may also help invigorate tomatoes.

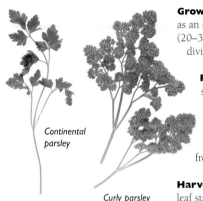

Continental parsley

Curly parsley

Growing habit Biennial grown as an annual; height 8–12 inches (20–30 cm); leaves are finely divided, on a long stalk.

Flowering time Early spring of second year; tiny, greenish yellow umbels.

Pest and disease prevention Usually free from pests and diseases.

Harvesting and storing Cut leaf stalks at the base for fresh foliage all summer. Hang in bunches to dry in shade, or freeze whole or chopped.

Special tips May go to seed prematurely if taproot severely damaged during transplanting. Dried parsley quickly loses flavor. Save a winter's worth by chopping and freezing fresh parsley in zippered plastic bags.

dead leaves. For productive plants, side-dress with compost in midseason. Usually survives the winter, but quickly goes to flower in spring. In order to attract beneficial insects to the garden, let a few plants flower and go to seed. Plants may be grown in pots to bring indoors for winter harvests.

HERBS AT HAND
Parsley is handy in pots near the kitchen; after the new plant is established, you can harvest the bright green sprigs as needed.

PASSIONFLOWER
Passiflora incarnata Passifloraceae

This climbing perennial with yellow, edible fruit has medicinal uses, but is usually grown as an ornamental for its unusual blossoms. It is also often found growing wild along fences and at the edges of woodland.

Best climate and site Zones 8–10 or frost-free greenhouse in cooler areas. Provide shade in strong sunlight.

Ideal soil conditions Fairly fertile but not rich well-drained, deep soil.

Growing guidelines Propagate by seed or summer cuttings. Mulch the soil each spring with a thin layer of compost. Prune to size in winter or early spring.

Growing habit Height 25–30 feet (7.5–9 m); hairy vine grows from a woody stem; it has coiling tendrils which it wraps around a support in order to climb. The leaves are deeply three-lobed.

Flowering time Early to late summer; sweet-scented, white or lavender petals and pink to purple

HEALING POWER
Passionflower has some properties that can act as a sedative and some that can be stimulating, which is why only professional herbalists should use the plant medicinally. It is fine to rub a few crushed leaves on minor cuts prior to applying first aid; it may be soothing.

Well-watered plants produce sweet fruit.

banded filaments. The flowers are followed by an edible, oval fruit that ranges in color from yellow to orange.

Pest and disease prevention
Usually free from pests and diseases; check occasionally.

Harvesting and storing
Collect the fruit in summer when ripe. It is best eaten fresh; the juice can be used to flavor drinks. The leaves and flowers are used medicinally for recurrent insomnia, but should not be taken without professional advice.

RELIGIOUS HISTORY
In the 17th century, the Spanish colonists of South America believed that Christ's crucifixion was represented in the design of the passionflower blossom; they saw it as a blessing on their efforts to convert the native people to Christianity.

PENNYROYAL

Mentha pulegium Labiatae

European pennyroyal is an attractive, low-maintenance groundcover that has a pleasant, mint-like fragrance and repels insects. It can be grown between paving stones in courtyards, in rockeries or even as a lawn.

Best climate and site Zones 5–9. Full sun though some shade tolerated.

Ideal soil conditions Ordinary, but always moist soil.

Growing guidelines Sow seed shallowly and thickly outdoors in early spring; thin to 6 inches (15 cm). Or take cuttings from stems, which easily root at joints. Divide old plants in spring or fall.

Growing habit Perennial; mat-forming with flowering, square stems, 6–12 inches (15–30 cm) tall. Slightly hairy, grayish-green leaves with serrated edges.

INTERNATIONAL HERB
Early colonists brought European pennyroyal to America for medicinal use but found that the Native Americans were already using a local species for the same purpose.

Flowering time July to August; reddish purple to lilac blossoms in whorled spikes.

Pest and disease prevention Usually free from pests and diseases; reported to repel insects.

Harvesting and storing Harvest foliage just before blooming, then hang in bunches to dry; store in an airtight container.

Special tips A powder made from the dried leaves keeps pets free from fleas.

Precautions Unsafe when taken internally; can be fatal.

PAIN RELIEF
Crush pennyroyal leaves and rub them on your skin to repel insects while you work in the garden. Folk healers suggest a garland of fresh pennyroyal leaves to relieve headaches.

PIPSISSEWA

Chimaphila umbellata Pyrolaceae

Pipsissewa is an ingredient in root beer, and has been used medicinally for hundred of years. It is a member of the heath family and grows mainly in the coniferous forests of the north.

Best climate and site Zones 5–8. Partial shade.

Ideal soil conditions Prefers humus-rich, moist but well-drained soil.

Growing guidelines Propagate by division of older plants, or take cuttings from rhizomes. It is best to divide in spring, and to take cuttings in fall. Grow cuttings in a cool greenhouse in a mixture of sand and peat moss. Mulch established plants with pine needles to maintain acid pH and soil moisture. Not easy to grow.

Growing habit Height to 10 inches (25 cm); low-growing evergreen; shoots from a creamy yellow, woody rhizome under ground; slightly crooked stems that trail along the ground; thick, glossy, obovate leaves to 2 inches (5 cm) long.

Flowering time May to August; long stalks topped by white or pink blossoms; five rounded, concave petals; flowers to ½ inch (1.5 cm) across; a few together in small terminal clusters; followed by egg-shaped capsules containing many seeds.

Pest and disease prevention Usually free from pests and diseases; check occasionally.

Harvesting and storing Harvest leaves for medicinal and culinary uses in late summer or early fall; store in an airtight container. Tea made with pipsissewa leaves has a good reputation as a natural remedy for kidney and urinary problems.

Special tips The flavor of pipsissewa leaves is both bitter and sweet. An infusion of the boiled leaves can produce perspiration (and for this reason the herb was used by both Native American and early settlers to treat typhus). Its first use in the United States to relieve the pain of rheumatism and to treat kidney disorders was during the Civil War. The general strength that is recommended is one teaspoon

of chopped leaves steeped in ½ cup of boiled water. Strain and sip the infusion, hot or cold, through the day; it is gentle enough to use several times a week.

Other common names Prince's pine, king's cure, ground holly, noble pine, pine tulip, waxflower, love-in-winter, bitter wintergreen, fragrant wintergreen, butter winter, rheumatism weed and pyrole. Its Latin name comes from the Greek words for winter and love.

HARD TO GROW

Pipsissewa is difficult to cultivate outside the pine forests where it grows wild. Provided with the moist, well-drained acidic soil it needs, it may thrive as a weed on a shaded lawn. Try it in a rock garden where the rocks and larger plants will provide shade and will help to retain moisture. Or grow it on the banks of a shady pond or river.

PLANTAIN, GREAT

Plantago major Plantaginaceae

Plantain is a common weed found in lawns, fields and roadsides. Try its tender, young leaves in salads, or steam and eat them like spinach. It was once considered to be an indispensible cure-all.

Best climate and site Zones 5–9. Full sun to partial shade. Plantain is a cool-climate herb; it may not thrive in tropical or sub-tropical climates.

Ideal soil conditions Grows in any well-drained soil.

Growing guidelines Sow seed shallowly outdoors in early spring or fall. Plantain flourishes in most conditions and requires little care.

Growing habit Perennial; height 6–18 inches (15–45 cm); broad, oval-shaped leaves with blunted ends and prominent veins. It forms rosettes near the ground and spreads quickly. It is short-lived and grows quickly from seed, so it can be treated as an annual.

Flowering time June to September; tall cylindrical spikes of many small, purplish green to yellowish green flowers. Bloom is followed by the appearance of small capsules which may contain as many as 25 seeds.

Pest and disease prevention Usually free from pests and diseases; check occasionally.

Harvesting and storing Use fresh leaves in salads, or for medicinal purposes such as treating bee stings and insect bites. Dig roots in fall, scrub them well and allow to dry until brittle. Chew the root to relieve toothache, or use with the rest of the plant to make a gold or camel-colored dye using an alum mordant.

Special tips From early times, plantain has been used in the treatment of everything from fevers to piles. Plantain leaves contain astringent and mucilage tannins which can help to speed up the healing of wounds, minor burns, bruises and poisonous bites. The crushed leaves can be applied directly onto the skin to soothe bites and stings from insects and rashes from plants such as poison-ivy rash; the fleshier the leaf, the more effective it is. Use it in an ointment base as a remedy for piles; make a poultice or compress of pulverized leaves for use on boils. For culinary use, only the young leaves should be harvested; the mature leaves are tough and fibrous. It is possible that the leaves will have a mildly laxative effect. Plantain is rarely planted for its ornamental qualities, but the small and variegated varieties can be an attractive addition to lawns and rockeries.

Other common names White man's foot, broad-leaved plantain, Englishman's foot, waybread.

A SHADY LIFE

Plantain is a particularly adaptable herb and, unlike most herbs, will grow well in areas where it is in some shade. Its companions in areas that are less exposed to sunlight include the medicinal herbs chamomile, comfrey and hyssop, and the culinary herbs, parsley, thyme and tarragon.

RED CLOVER

Trifolium pratense Leguminosae

Red clover is a member of the legume family. With the aid of microscopic soil organisms, these legumes add nitrogen, an important element for all plant growth, to the soil.

The flower tops are used in herbal preparations.

Best climate and site Zones 6–9. Full sun, partial shade tolerated.

Ideal soil conditions Light, sandy garden soil.

Growing guidelines Broadcast or drill seed shallowly in early spring for a cover crop. Thin plants to 1 foot (30 cm) apart.

Growing habit Perennial; height 1–2 feet (30–60 cm); leaflets oval, hairy.

Flowering time Mid- to late summer; bright pinkish-purple, fragrant, ovoid heads.

Pest and disease prevention Usually free from pests and diseases; can be susceptible to "clover sickness" in which toxins released by the roots stop the plant from growing.

LIVING MULCH
Red clover can be grown as a living mulch or a green manure crop. The flowers attract beneficial insects, and the nitrogen-fixing bacteria on the roots work to enhance soil fertility.

Red clover tea is slightly sweet and mildly sedative.

Harvesting and storing
Collect flowers at full bloom and dry on paper in the shade; store in airtight containers. Use to make a slightly sweet tea that is said to relieve irritating coughs.

Special tips Sow as a cover crop to renew the soil between demanding crops or use as a permanent groundcover.

ROSEMARY
Rosmarinus officinalis Labiatae

The flowers and leaves of this highly scented herb are used to season and garnish food. Rosemary is also favored by herbalists as an insect repellent, a hair and scalp tonic and a breath freshener.

Best climate and site Zones 7–9. Grown outdoors where temperatures remain above 10°F (-12°C). Full sun to partial shade.

Ideal soil conditions Light, well-drained soil.

ORNAMENTAL BUSH
Gardeners in warm climates—especially the Pacific Southwest, where rosemary reaches shrub proportions—can enjoy this attractive, aromatic plant in pots or as a hedge or border. Never allow container plantings to dry out; rosemary does not recover from severe wilting.

Growing guidelines Sow seed shallowly indoors in early spring, then transplant to pots outdoors; plant out to garden for second season, spacing 3 feet (90 cm) apart. Or take cuttings from new growth in fall, or layer the stems in spring. Overwintering success varies with local conditions and cultivar; larger plants may overwinter better outdoors than small ones. Potted plants may be brought into a sunny greenhouse for the winter; or keep them at 45°F (7°C) in a sunny garage or enclosed porch, watering infrequently.

Growing habit Height 2–6 feet (60–180 cm); tender perennial with scaly bark and aromatic, needlelike leaves.

Flowering time Spring and summer, Small pale blue to pink tubular flowers in axillary clusters.

Pest and disease prevention

Indoors, watch for scale pests and wipe them from the foliage with cotton soaked with rubbing alcohol.

Harvesting and storing

Snip fresh foliage as needed all year.

Rosemary oil is used in massage and baths to help relieve insomnia, stress, tension and to treat scalp problems.

FRIEND TO VEGETABLES

Rosemary is a popular companion for cabbage, broccoli and related crops, as well as carrots and onions. The fragrance is said to repel insects; companion gardeners use it for cabbage flies, root maggot flies and other flying pests. The small flowers will attract large numbers of bees.

Special tips Use sprigs of rosemary as a dry marinade for meats and poultry. An infusion of the leaves can be used as a hair rinse and as a mouth wash; sip it warm to improve digestion.

Other species and varieties

❖ Prostrate rosemary (*R. prostratus*): Some cultivars have deep blue flowers almost all year; good for rock gardens and hanging baskets; not very winter-hardy.
❖ White-flowered rosemary (*R. officinalis* var. *alba*): Showy blossoms; a hardy variety.

ROSES (DOG, CABBAGE, PROVENCE)

Rosa spp. Rosaceae

The aromatic flowers and fruit of these attractive shrubs have medicinal properties and are used for making perfume. Different species bloom in white, yellow, pink or red in varying shapes, sizes and growing habits.

Best climate and site Zones 6–9. Full sun to partial shade.

Ideal soil conditions Well-drained, ideally clayey soil.

Growing guidelines Propagate from seed, or cuttings. Purchase nursery stock for best results. Work in plenty of compost or well-rotted manure when planting, and mulch each spring. Plant approximately 30 inches (75 cm) apart in beds. Lightly prune in winter to maintain shape.

ROSY HEALTH
Rose oil, distilled from the petals, is used to relieve headaches, insomnia and nervous tension. Rosehip tea, made from the fruit of the rose, is very high in Vitamin C.

Roses need at least six hours of sun each day.

Growing habit Perennial; height varies with species; stems thorned and upright to spreading.

Flowering time Summer; single or double, often clustered flowers with berry-like hips, or fruit, ripening in fall.

Pest and disease prevention Knock aphids and mites from leaves with a spray of water. Handpick large pests daily.

Harvesting and storing Gather the petals before they are completely open and dry them quickly on screens or paper.

PLANT ANEW
As with all members of the rose family, never plant a new rose in an old rose's "grave." Disease pathogens or allelopathic substances that hinder the growth of a new plant of the same genus may be lurking in the soil.

RUE

Ruta graveolens Rutaceae

Rue has a pungent, skunk-like odor. Rose growers sometimes recommend strong-smelling rue as a companion planting to repel insect pests. In the garden, its bluish foliage contrasts well with the greens of other plants.

Best climate and site Zones 6–9. Full sun.

Ideal soil conditions Poor, well-drained soil.

Growing guidelines Sow seed shallowly indoors in late winter, transplanting outdoors in late spring 18–24 inches (45–60 cm) apart. Take cuttings from new growth or divide older plants. Grows well in a pot and continues growing when wintered indoors by a sunny window. Mulch with compost each spring, and prune away dead stems.

RUE TONICS
Rue cream is used to treat insect bites, gout, rheumatism and sciatica. Professionally prepared tonics may be taken internally to soothe gas pains and to improve digestion.

Growing habit Perennial; height 2–3 feet (60–90 cm); woody stems with greenish blue foliage.

Flowering time Summer to early fall; yellow-green blossoms in terminal clusters.

Pest and disease prevention Generally free from pests and diseases; check occasionally.

Harvesting and storing Harvest several times each season, bunching foliage to dry. Use the dried seedpods and leaves for flower arrangements.

Special tips According to folklore, rue slows the growth of basil, sage, cabbage and broccoli.

Precautions Rue has a longer list of enemies than it does of partners, beginning with the gardener. Merely brushing against it can cause an unpleasant and painful contact dermatitis in susceptible individuals. Unfortunately, you won't know if you're susceptible until you experience the blistering rash. Overexposure to sunlight after taking rue internally may result in severe sunburn. It should never be taken by pregnant women and should only ever be taken in small amounts and on the advice of a professional herbalist.

Other common names Herb of grace.

CONTRASTING HUES

The striking blue-green foliage of this perennial herb has an unusual and distinctive fragrance. Rue is a beautiful, eye-catching plant for the herb garden. It is also good in pots, especially terra cotta, which sets off the lacy foliage.

SAFFLOWER

Carthamus tinctorius Compositae

The orange-yellow flowers of safflower are used to produce the yellow and red dyes used in facial makeup such as rouge. A popular cooking oil is manufactured from the seeds.

Best climate and site Zones 6–10. Full sun.

Ideal soil conditions Dry, poor to average, well-drained soil.

Growing guidelines Sow seed shallowly outdoors in spring; thin to 6 inches (15 cm). Safflower transplants poorly.

Growing habit Annual; height 2–3 feet (60–90 cm); upright stems branch at the top; spiny, oval leaves along a stiff, smooth, whitish stem which branches out towards the top.

Flowering time Summer; orange to yellow, compound thistle-like flowers. Followed by small, shiny, white fruit.

Pest and disease prevention Handpick snails and slugs from seedlings. Usually free from other pests and diseases.

Harvesting and storing Collect flowers for drying in the morning, before they are fully open. Wrap a rubber band around a bunch of six to eight stems and hang upside down in a shaded, airy spot. The dried flowers retain their color well; add them to potpourri and to dried herb and flower bouquets or use them to make dyes for silk, wool, food and cosmetics.

Special tips The seed of the safflower plant is high in linoleic acid, an essential fatty acid, which can help to lower cholesterol in the blood and prevent heart disease. Infuse the

Safflower oil is good to use in cooking, when no taste should be imparted to the food.

flowers by steeping in boiled water for a tea that will soothe skin problems and act as a laxative and diuretic. Use the dried flowers as you would use saffron for coloring foods such as sauces, soups, marinades, pasta, curries and rice. Use about five times the amount of saffron you would use. It cannot be used to substitute for the taste of saffron; it's bland by comparison. You may have some success increasing the flavor by crushing the flowers onto a cutting board with the back of a spoon or a rolling pin.

Precautions Don't drink safflower tea during pregnancy.

ANCIENT PLANTS
Safflower plants have been cultivated as far back as the time of the pharaohs in Egypt when they were used for their oil. Originally safflower grew wild in Europe, Asia and probably Egypt.

SAFFRON

Crocus sativus Iridaceae

The fragrant pink, mauve and purple blooms of saffron with their red stigmas and long, yellow anthers are a striking and valuable addition to the garden; saffron is the source of a yellow dye and unique, delicate culinary flavoring.

Best climate and site Zones 6–9. Best in full sun, sheltered from winds and frost.

Ideal soil conditions
Light, fertile, well-drained soil.

Growing guidelines
Plant saffron corms 3–4 inches (7.5–10 cm) deep, with the rooting side down, in early fall at 4–6-inch (10–15-cm) intervals. Lift and divide corms every two to three years, after the foliage has died down in spring or fall. Self-propagates.

PRECIOUS HARVEST
The dried, dark yellow "threads" of the saffron flower are used in cooking. The flowers are picked at dawn and the stigmas are removed by hand.

Growing habit Perennial; height 3½–6 inches (8–15 cm); grasslike leaves.

Flowering time Fall; flowers arise from soil without stems.

Pest and disease prevention
Usually free from pests and diseases, but after cool wet summers may flower poorly.

Harvesting and storing
Collect individual stigmas; dry on paper away from breezes; store in an airtight, glass container in a cool, dry place away from direct light. The flowers can be dried whole.

Special tips Good quality saffron is expensive to buy because the crops yield so little product; there is a short blooming period of about 20 days, and from 160,000 saffron flowers, just over 11 pounds

(5 kg) of stigmas are obtained which, once dried, produce only about 2 pounds (1 kg) of saffron. Stored properly, good quality saffron will keep for about two years. Imitation and poor quality saffron products are widely available; you can tell the difference by the price and by the speed with which the product dyes the food it's mixed with. The color of true saffron takes a few minutes to develop whereas the color of imitation saffron appears instantly. Soak saffron threads in hot water or stock before adding to food so that the color spreads evenly.

STUNNING LANDSCAPE

Plant saffron randomly in areas of lawn that are not walked on regularly; the contrasting colors of their stigma and petals, combined with their lack of stem, make for a dramatic burst of beauty against the grassy backdrop. A similar effect can be achieved by planting saffron in rock gardens.

SAGE

Salvia officinalis Labiatae

Sage is an easy-to-grow, shrubby perennial with aromatic foliage used fresh and dried in cooking and in herbal medicines. Its velvety texture and small blue flowers add a soft accent to the garden.

Best climate and site Zones 6–9. Full sun to partial shade.

Ideal soil conditions
Well-drained garden soil.

Growing guidelines Sow seed shallowly outdoors in late spring or indoors in late winter; plant at 20–24 inches (50–60 cm) intervals. Trim back drastically in early spring to encourage vigorous, bushy new growth. Plants may decline after several years; take cuttings or divide in spring or fall to have a steady supply. Sage may improve the growth and flavor of

FAST GROWER
The plentiful, usually blue, flowers of this perennial herb are attractive to bees and other beneficial insects. Use sage as a border planting, or dot the plants among annual or perennial vegetables; they grow to an appreciable size in just one season.

cabbage, carrots, strawberries and tomatoes; it is also thought to grow well with marjoram. It may, however, stunt the growth of cucumbers, rue and onions.

Growing habit Height 1–2 feet (30–60 cm); woody stems have wrinkled gray-green foliage.

COMMERCIAL PRODUCT
Dried sage is usually sold in crumbled leaves or in a powdered form. The taste can be different to fresh sage, and to freshly dried sage; it may have less of a lemon flavor and be a little musty.

Flowering time Spring; tubular purple flowers in whorled spikes.

Pest and disease prevention Rarely bothered by pests and diseases.

Harvesting and storing Snip fresh leaves as needed, or bunch them and hang to dry for use during winter months. A branch of strongly aromatic sage is a fragrant addition to a sweater drawer or blanket chest, and it may help keep clothes moths away. Refrain from harvesting the first year.

Other species and cultivars
❖ Golden sage (*S. officinalis* 'Icterina'): Leaves variegated gold and green; excellent bushy border plant. *S. officinalis* 'Purpurascens' has the leaves flushed reddish-purple. *S. officinalis* 'Tricolor' produces foliage splashed creamy-white with tints of pink and

MOBILE REPELLENT
Some companion gardeners believe that sage deters cabbage-family pests such as imported cabbageworms and root maggot flies. Grow it in pots and move it around as needed.

purple; not quite so hardy.
❖ Pineapple sage (*S. elegans*): Height 24–42 inches (60–105 cm); dark green, pineapple-scented leaves; brilliant red tubular flowers.

SANTOLINA (LAVENDER COTTON)

Santolina chamaecyparissus Compositae

Santolina is an evergreen shrub with an aromatic scent. Though it is often called lavender cotton, it is a member of the daisy family. It is useful as an insect repellent.

Use sprigs of santolina in linen and clothes cupboards.

Best climate and site Zones 6–9. Full sun.

Ideal soil conditions Poor, well-drained soil. If the soil is too rich or too wet, the foliage may be dull and growth of the whole plant may be extremely slow.

Growing guidelines Transplant in spring after danger of frost. Take cuttings in late summer to early fall; layer, or divide older plants in spring. Set 2 feet (60 cm) apart; less for hedging. Shear or clip the plant in spring or summer; never in the colder months. Pinch off fading blooms in fall. Don't overwater.

Growing habit Height to 2 feet (60 cm); leaves silver-green, long, narrow, highly aromatic when crushed. Forms low mounds.

Flowering time Summer; yellow, button-like blooms rise above the foliage on 4–6-inch (10–15-cm) stalks; the fruit is a brownish pod. May not flower the first year.

Pest and disease prevention Usually free from pests and diseases; check occasionally.

Harvesting and storing Harvest and bunch the top 8–10 inches (20–25 cm) of foliage in summer, and hang to dry. Use as a backing for making aromatic wreaths and sprinkle into potpourri. Collect flowers with stem at full bloom; hang to dry.

Special tips Store the highly aromatic leaves with clothes to repel moths. Grow santolina along walkways and the borders of garden beds; its silvery foliage is so reflective that it will highlight the edges of paths and other plants at night. The coral shaped leaves make santolina an excellent plant for formal and knot gardens and for topiary designs. Santolina makes a lovely indoor ornamental; grow it in wide pots and clip to a shape if desired.

SHEAR PLEASURE

The bright yellow flowers of lavender cotton are striking when grown in masses. For use in smaller areas, you may want to forgo the flowers and shear the plants into a low hedge around patios, pathways and herb gardens, or for use in a formal garden.

SASSAFRAS

Sassafras albidum Lauraceae

Sassafras is a tall, deciduous, native American tree that produces an oil once used as a flavoring for cold and hot beverages. It has striking yellow, orange and red foliage in the fall.

Best climate and site Zones 5–9, sun or partial shade.

Ideal soil conditions Well-drained acid to neutral garden soil.

Growing guidelines Propagate by seed or by suckers which the roots send out. You can also take root cuttings. Only very small, young trees transplant successfully because the more mature trees have long taproots. You can grow the cuttings in small containers and move them to their permanent position once they are healthy and growing well.

Growing habit Height 20–60 feet (6–18 m); smooth, orange-brown bark with deep channels. Leaves are mostly three-lobed, downy and greatly varying in size. The young foliage smells of citrus; the roots and bark have a scent like root beer. Sassafras is found in eastern North America, from Michigan and south to Florida, and east to Texas.

Flowering time Spring; clusters of small, inconspicuous greenish yellow blossoms appear before the leaves. Male and female flowers are usually on separate trees. The fruit that follows is a pea-sized, dark blue to purple berry that contains one seed.

Pest and disease prevention Usually free from diseases; it can be affected by Japanese beetle and gypsy moth. Try a mulch of loose catnip branches in the soil around the young sassafras tree, or grow some catnip close by; many companion gardeners believe that the strong vapor from catnip repels Japanese beetles. If gypsy moths become a problem, try any brand of "BT" which is a microbial insecticide based on naturally occurring insect diseases.

Harvesting and storing Peel the bark off the tree and use as required or dry and store in an airtight container.

Special tips Sassafras bark and root bark has antiseptic properties; they can be made into a poultice, decoction or ointment and used externally to soothe itchiness and skin wounds. Grow sassafras in the shade where other trees will not grow; use it to provide shade for smaller plants that cannot tolerate full sun.

Precautions For hundreds of years the bark of the sassafras tree was used to make a soothing, aromatic tea, and until about thirty years ago, material from sassafras roots was used in the production of root beer; however studies have shown that when taken internally, sassafras may be carcinogenic.

HARDY AND COLORFUL
Sassafras used to be valued for its medicinal properties but is now grown mostly as an ornamental. It thrives in just about any conditions, including rocky soils and damp areas, and provides magnificent fall color as well as a wonderful, fresh scent.

SAVORY, WINTER
Satureja montana Labiatae

This aromatic, bushy, hardy perennial has a peppery flavor and has been used in cooking for 2,000 years. It is also thought to be beneficial for digestion and skin problems.

Best climate and site Zones 5–9. Full sun.

Ideal soil conditions Poor, well-drained soil.

Growing guidelines Sow seed shallowly outdoors in late spring, thinning to 1 foot (30 cm). Germinates slowly. Take cuttings, or divide older plants in spring or fall. Prune to stop woody growth.

Growing habit Height 6–12 inches (15–30 cm); branched, woody stems, oblong, needlelike leaves.

Flowering time June; pale purple blossoms.

Pest and disease prevention Usually free from pests and diseases. Check occasionally.

Harvesting and storing Harvest fresh as needed or cut and dry the foliage just before flowering. Use as a flavoring in a variety of dishes, teas, herb butters and vinegars. Use the flower tops as an astringent for oily skin or infuse it to make a tea that will stimulate the appetite and promote digestion. A strong infusion can also be used as a mouth wash. The fresh leaves can be bruised and rubbed on the skin to treat insect bites and stings.

Special tips Winter savory is commonly used as a flavoring

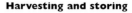

STRONG SCENT
Winter savory has a strong, almost pine-like fragrance. Old-time herbalists recommended adding dried, crushed winter savory to breadings for "meate." Sachets of dried savory can be used to repel moths from the clothes closet.

in commercially manufactured salami and other processed meats. Some companion gardeners plant the herb with beans and cabbage to deter pests. Winter savory is also said to improve the flavor and growth of onions.

Other species ❖ Summer savory (*S. hortensis*): Annual; prefers light, fertilized soil; transplants poorly; height 12–18 inches (30–45 cm); linear, downy leaves; pale lavender or white blossoms; used as an antiflatulent.

A SAVORY CHRISTMAS
Winter savory is lower growing than its summer cousin. Its thin leaves are a glossy dark green, adding some contrast to herb garden plantings. Plant it near the kitchen door, so it's in easy reach for cooking. The leaves hold well into winter, so you can snip them as needed, sometimes even through to Christmas time.

SOAPWORT
Saponaria officinalis Caryophyllaceae

This hardy perennial is a localized roadside weed, sometimes also found on railway banks and waste land. It is a pretty, trailing plant with white or pink blossoms in spring. As its name implies, soapwort lathers and cleans like soap.

Best climate and site Zones 5–9. Full sun to light shade.

Ideal soil conditions Average to poor, well-drained soil.

Growing guidelines Divide established plants in fall or early spring. Plant after the danger of hard frost has passed, in early spring. Soapwort may be started indoors, about six weeks before last frost. Water regularly until the plants are established; it is very drought tolerant once it has matured. After the flowers have faded in mid-summer, clip it right back; this will force another flowering stage. Don't plant soapwort next to fishponds; its lathering properties may seep into the water and poison the fish.

Growing habit Height 1–2 feet (30–60 cm); sturdy branching stem that runs to purple-green at the base. Soapwort spreads by seed and by runners. The leaves are oval, pointed and pale green; their sap contains saponin, which is the substance that creates a lather when boiled. The strength of the scent is affected by where the plant is grown.

Flowering time July to September; pink to white, five-petaled or often double flowers in terminal clusters.

Pest and disease prevention Usually free from pests and diseases; check occasionally.

Harvesting and storing Harvest fresh roots and leaves as needed. Clean, chop and boil the root to make a sudsy solution. Use a juicer or wring a large quantity of leaves to produce a juice that can be used to soothe irritated or infected skin.

Special tips Dried soapwort lathers less and has less scent than the fresh plant; the aroma is a little like cloves. Boil the fresh roots and leaves to form a soapy lather that can be used to wash hair, old or delicate fabrics and pets. The leaves can also be used when washing clothes to soften the water; in the past, soapwort was considered an essential plant in dyeing because the roots were used to wash yarn before it was dyed. Use pressed and dried soapwort flowers in in herbal craft, such as floral candles. Soapwort was a feature of the medicines of many cultures, but in recent times it has been found to be toxic to humans and animals and is only used externally in herbal healing. A juice extracted from the leaves or roots may stop itching and heal skin problems.

SWEET SOOTHER

Soapwort is a lovely ornamental with a sweet, slightly fruity fragrance that perfumes the early evening air. It is easy to cultivate and, once established, needs little care other than to keep it from self-sowing. If you're bitten by an insect in the garden, crush a few leaves and rub them on the bite.

SORREL

Rumex acetosa Polygonaceae

In the spring, use sorrel's tender new leaves to make a delicate soup or a sauce for fish, or add them to salad greens. Grown in meadows, the summer stalks of sorrel's reddish-green flowers will make the whole area appear to be tinted red.

Best climate and site Zones 5–9. Full sun.

Ideal soil conditions
Moderately fertile moist garden soil.

Growing guidelines Sow seed shallowly outdoors in late spring, thinning to 18 inches (45 cm). Or divide older plants in early spring or fall. If planting late, try to plant about two months before the first fall frost to give the roots enough time to establish before the soil freezes. Since the weather may be hot when you are planting, water

HERBS FOR WINTER
Late summer and early fall can be an excellent time to plant perennial herbs like sorrel. Plant it with chives, garlic, oregano, sage, thyme and winter savory. Companion flowers that adapt well to fall planting include asters and chrysanthemums.

Sorrel produces a whorled, reddish flower.

the sorrel thoroughly and often; mulching will help the soil to retain moisture.

Growing habit Hardy perennial; height 30–36 inches (75–90 cm); wavy, green leaves. Spreads by creeping roots and stems; takes a lot of hand-weeding to eliminate.

Flowering time Midsummer; greenish yellow to red flowers.

Pest and disease prevention Usually free from pests and diseases; check occasionally.

Harvesting and storing Harvest the outside leaves regularly to promote new growth. Sorrel leaves are best eaten fresh, but can be blanched and frozen.

Precautions Sorrel should not be eaten by anyone suffering from rheumatism, arthritis or gout.

WONDER JUICE
Sorrel leaves can be used in cooking just as spinach would be used. Juice from the leaf can also be used to bleach rust, mold, grass and ink stains from linen and wicker. Sorrel tea may sooth mouth ulcers and skin wounds.

Species ❖ French sorrel (*R. scutatus*): Lower-growing perennial; triangular pale green leaves with silvery patches; more bitter flavor.

SOUTHERNWOOD

Artemisia abrotanum Compositae

This ornamental and hardy perennial was once used as an aphrodisiac and to stimulate the growth of men's beards. These days it is considered more useful as an ornamental.

Best climate and site Zones 5–9. Full sun.

Ideal soil conditions Well-drained garden soil. Don't fertilize; southernwood prefers a lean diet.

Growing guidelines Buy a young plant or propagate by cuttings; you can also divide older plants in spring or fall. Space the plants 2–4 feet (60–120 cm) apart. Southernwood is very difficult to grow from seed, but cuttings root easily. In early spring, prune back hard to shape. Grow as a pest-repelling border, or interplant it in permanent spots throughout the vegetable garden and orchard. Unlike wormwood, its less pleasantly scented relative, southernwood doesn't generally harm the growth of any plant.

Growing habit Height 3–6 feet (1–1.8 m); finely divided, gray-green leaves. It is native to southern Europe and has been naturalized in the United States.

Flowering time August; small, inconspicuous button-like yellow-white blossoms (rarely blooms in northern climates).

Pest and disease prevention Usually free from pests and diseases; check occasionally.

Harvesting and storing Collect foliage anytime in summer and hang in bunches to dry. Use dried foliage to repel moths in stored clothing, or as an aromatic backing for herbal wreaths. Southernwood tea may aid digestion, treat worms and relieve catarrh. You can also use an infusion of the leaves as a fragrance for the bath and as a rinse for hair. Freshly harvested foliage is a nice addition to floral arrangements. The yellow stem of southernwood is used to make a yellow dye for wool.

Special tips Plant southernwood in the back of borders to give height or grow as a light hedge. Companion gardeners recommend interplanting southernwood as a kind of living insect repellent. Planted among beans, it's said to deter black aphids; near broccoli, cabbage and related crops it's reputed to repel cabbage moths and other pests. The herb is also said to deter codling moths from orchard fruit. Its sharp, acid scent is invigorating which is why it had a reputation as a general stimulant; if you're tired, hang a sprig in the car or take it to work.

Other common names The lover's plant, old-man, lad's love, maid's ruin.

CONTRASTING BACKDROP
Use this perennial herb throughout the garden. Its feathery leaves stay fresh in the heat and provide a soft backdrop for brightly colored flowers. The sharp, lemony scent is pleasant on a deck or patio. Pinch off a leaf, bruise it and rub it on your arms and legs to release the essential oils that keep insects away.

241

SWEET CICELY
Myrrhis odorata Umbelliferae

Sweet cicely has a scent like lovage and a sweet licorice taste. The leaves can be used fresh in salads and the root can be cooked. It is also a lovely and hardy ornamental with numerous blooms.

Best climate and site Zones 5–9. Partial shade.

Ideal soil conditions Rich, humusy, well-drained soil; pH 6.0–6.7.

Growing guidelines Sow seed shallowly outdoors in late spring, thinning to 2 feet (60 cm); germination is slow; self-sows. Divide older plants in spring or fall, leaving each new piece with a bud. Mulch each spring with compost or well-rotted manure.

YEAR-ROUND ORNAMENTAL
The lacy leaves and masses of white blossoms make sweet cicely useful as a single planting, or in mixed flower beds where it will contrast with and highlight colored spring and summer blooms. When it has finished flowering, the fruit will make an interesting addition to winter bouquets.

Growing habit Perennial; height to 3 feet (90 cm); leaves are fernlike, finely divided; whitish, velvety and spotted underneath. Native to Europe; naturalized in North America.

Flowering time May to June; plentiful white blossoms in compound umbels; the inner blooms are male and the outer blooms are bisexual. Followed by a shiny, chocolate-colored fruit to 1 inch (2.5 cm) long with ridged seeds that have an anise flavor.

WORTH THE TIME

Sweet cicely is difficult to propagate and can be hard to germinate from seed; it's better to purchase seedlings. Though you need to take care with the young plants, it's worth persisting with the introduction of this herb into your garden. Once established, it will self-sow and provide culinary and visual delights in the years to come.

Pest and disease prevention Usually free from pests and diseases.

Harvesting and storing Use fresh leaves as needed all summer in salads and cooking. One plant yields about four cups of leaves and half a cup of seeds. Collect seed heads and dry on paper in a shady spot; store in airtight containers. Use the seeds in cakes, candy, syrups, liqueurs and desserts. Dig roots after the first year, scrub and dry until brittle or use them fresh like parsnips.

Special tips Use in any recipes with carrots, parsnips, turnips, brussel sprouts, cabbage, potatoes; it nicely flavors cream for fish sauces and adds an unusual touch to stewed fruit and fruit pies.

Other common names Myrrh, anise, sweet chervil.

SWEET WOODRUFF

Galium odoratum Rubiaceae

Sweet woodruff is a hardy perennial groundcover that grows well in full shade and smells like vanilla when dried. In the past, garlands of woodruff were hung in homes and churches.

Best climate and site Zones 5–9. Prefers some shade; grows well under trees. The color of the leaf will fade in full sun.

Ideal soil conditions Moist, humusy, well-drained, soil; pH 5.0–8.0. It can tolerate a slightly poorer soil.

Growing guidelines Sow ripe seed in shallow, moist, shaded soil in late summer or early fall outdoors; germination may take as long as 200 days. Purchase plants from nurseries and plant in spring, 6–9 inches (15–23 cm) apart; divide the creeping rootstock of established plants after flowering is finished, in spring or fall. Sweet woodruff is not suitable for growing indoors.

Growing habit Height 8–12 inches (20–30 cm).

Flowering time May to June; small, funnel-shaped, white blossoms.

Pest and disease prevention Usually free from pests and diseases; the essential oil has insect-repellent properties.

Harvesting and storing Gather foliage and flowering stems anytime in summer; hang in bunches in a warm, airy place to dry. Store the leaves whole to preserve the scent. A tan-colored dye can be produced from the stems and leaves; the roots will produce a red dye.

Special tips Sweet woodruff is unusual among the aromatic herbs because the leaves only develop their sweet, distinctive scent of fresh-cut hay and vanilla when dried. The vanilla aroma comes from a constituent called coumarin, which is also in tonka beans and the herb melilot. Coumarin is commonly and commercially used in the production of perfumes. The dried leaves can be used as a fixative in potpourri or in sachets to repel moths and other insects from linen, clothes, mattresses and rugs.

Use also in herbal pillows for its soothing scent. Pick and bruise a few fresh leaves to apply to stings, bites and minor wounds. Use the flowering stem to make fresh garlands. Add the herb to young wine to enhance and deepen the flavor; place a few fresh sprigs in the bottle for two days.

Precautions May be toxic when taken internally, except when used in alcoholic beverages. Must not be used in excessive quantities; it can cause dizziness and vomiting, and may be carcinogenic.

SHY HERB
In folklore, sweet woodruff was said to signify humility because it grows as though it were shy, keeping close to the ground. It makes a wonderful, low-maintenance carpet of rich green in shaded areas. Use it especially in large, wooded areas where it will thrive under the canopy of trees.

TANSY

Tanacetum vulgare Compositae

This easy-to-grow, aromatic and attractive perennial has brilliant green foliage and yellow button-like flowers. Companion gardeners recommend tansy to improve the vigor of roses and bramble fruits, and to repel pests.

Best climate and site Zones 6–9. Full sun to partial shade.

Ideal soil conditions Well-drained garden soil; pH 6.0–7.0.

Growing guidelines Sow seed shallowly in late winter indoors; transplant outdoors after danger of frost, 4 feet (1.2 m) apart. Divide established plants in spring or fall. Spreads easily. Prune vigorously in midsummer for lush growth in late fall. Plants may need support; they will stand upright when grown along fences.

THE GOOD AND THE BAD

The yellow, button-like flowers of tansy attract butterflies and insects to the garden, including beneficials and predators. Studies have indicated some reduction in the numbers of squash bugs and Colorado potato beetles on crops interplanted with tansy, but researchers also noted an increase in imported cabbageworms.

Growing habit Height 3–4 feet (90–120 cm); erect, branched stems with fernlike leaves that are aromatic when touched. Tansy grows and spreads very fast, even in poor soil.

Flowering time July to September: button-like, yellow blossoms in terminal clusters.

Pest and disease prevention Usually free from pests and diseases. Aphids may be a problem in some northern locations; to control, dislodge them with a spray of water.

Harvesting and storing Collect foliage anytime during summer and hang in bunches to dry. Flowers dry well and remain yellow, but lose their brightness; they are excellent in dried arrangements. Use the leaves and flowers to make green-gold dye.

Use flowers in dried flower arrangements.

Special tips Tansy is said to repel certain pest insects, such as Japanese beetles and flea beetles, while attracting the beneficials.

Precautions Tansy was formerly popular in herbalists' remedies, but its use can cause violent reactions and death. A toxin called thujone is the culprit; it is also found in wormwood.

OVERCROWDING PROBLEM
Fast-growing tansy can quickly get out of hand in the loose, rich soil of the garden. Any benefits of companion planting tansy with other crops could be canceled out by the overcrowding effect of the tansy. If you want to grow tansy with other crops, consider planting it in a bottomless bucket sunk into the soil.

TARRAGON, FRENCH

Artemisia dracunculus var. sativa Compositae

French tarragon's heavy licorice flavor holds well in cooking. Make sure not to buy Russian tarragon; it is a lanky plant with none of the signature licorice fragrance of the French herb.

Best climate and site Zones 6–9. Full sun to partial shade.

Ideal soil conditions Well-drained garden soil.

Growing guidelines Cannot be grown from seed (only Russian tarragon can be grown from seed). Take basal cuttings of new growth in spring or fall. Divide older plants in late winter every three years; space 12–24 inches (30–60 cm) apart. Prune away flower stems each year, for most vigorous growth and best flavor. To grow indoors in winter, pot young plants in summer, cutting foliage to just above the soil. Seal pot in a plastic bag and refrigerate to mimic winter. In fall, unwrap and place in a sunny window for winter harvests.

INDOOR OUTDOOR
Tarragon adapts well to life in a container, either outside or inside on a sunny windowsill. French tarragon is obtainable only in pots. Make sure the plant gets good air circulation.

Growing habit Height 2–4 feet (60–120 cm); hardy perennial with long, branched green stems.

Flowering time Late summer; small, round greenish-yellow flowers. French tarragon will only flower in warm climates.

Pest and disease prevention Generally free from pests and diseases; check occasionally.

Harvesting and storing Clip foliage as needed all summer, or indoors in winter. Foliage may be harvested entirely twice each summer. Fresh foliage lasts several weeks in the refrigerator when wrapped in paper towels, then placed in a plastic bag. Bunch and hang to dry away from sunlight. May also be preserved in vinegars or frozen in zippered plastic bags.

Special tips Rub a leaf and sniff before you buy; the licorice scent (and flavor) is evident only in the French type. Use sparingly—the flavor of this herb is very strong.

COMPANION TO VEGETABLES
Place a tarragon plant at the corners of raised beds, grow it in the herb garden, or interplant it among plots of vegetables. It is one of the aromatic herbs recommended by companion gardeners to improve the growth and flavor of neighboring vegetables.

THYME, COMMON OR GARDEN
Thymus vulgaris Labiatae

Easy-growing thyme is a favorite of cooks and gardeners. Delicately pretty in leaf and flower, a carpet of thyme makes a beautiful underplanting for roses. It enriches the flavor of meats and soups.

Best climate and site Zones 6–9. Ideally in full sun but partial shade tolerated.

Ideal soil conditions Ordinary, well-drained soil.

Growing guidelines Sow seed shallowly in late winter indoors, keeping the soil at 70°F (21°C) for best germination. Plant outdoors in late spring in clumps, 1 foot (30 cm) apart. You can divide older plants in spring or take cuttings in late summer or fall. In winter, mulch with a light material like straw. Replace plants every three to four years to control woody growth.

TIME OUT FOR PESTS
Companion gardeners recommend planting thyme with just about everything in the garden; it is said to improve flavor and repel pests. A spray of thyme will also deter insects.

Growing habit Height 6–15 inches (15–38 cm); hardy evergreen shrublet; woody stems; tiny gray-green, aromatic leaves.

Flowering time Midsummer; tubular lilac to pink blossoms in clusters on the tips of the stems.

Pest and disease prevention Generally free from pests and diseases; check occasionally.

Harvesting and storing Snip foliage as needed during the summer, or harvest entirely twice per season, leaving at least 3 inches (7.5) of growth. Bunch together and hang to dry, or first strip the leaves and dry on a screen. Foliage freezes well in airtight containers or bags.

Related plants ❖ Mother of thyme (*T. praecox* subsp. *arcticus*): Height to 4 inches (10 cm); forms a dense mat 16–25 inches (40–60 cm) across; flower color (rose, purple, crimson or white) varies with cultivar.
❖ Lemon thyme (*T. x citriodorus*): Height to 5–10 inches (13–25 cm); leaves are dark green or white or yellow variegated, glossy and lemon-scented; not grown from seed; especially tasty with fish or chicken.

Use a sprig of thyme as a garnish.

DRY BENEFITS
Thyme leaves dry well and are less pungent than the fresh foliage, so there is less danger of overpowering food.

VALERIAN, COMMON
Valeriana officinalis Valerianaceae

Formerly much used in Nordic countries, this plant has powerful medicinal properties. It has been prized for centuries as a tranquilizer and drugs based upon the herb are still used today in some European countries.

The leaves give off a sharp scent.

Best climate and site Zones 6–9. Full sun to partial shade.

SWEET DREAMS
Valerian tea may be helpful as a sedative for mild insomnia, and as pain relief for headaches and cramps.

Ideal soil conditions Fertile, moist garden soil.

Growing guidelines Sow seed shallowly outdoors in April, transplanting to the garden when small plants are established. Germinates poorly. Propagate by division in spring or fall, spacing new plants 1 foot (30 cm) apart. Plants quickly become crowded, so dig and renew them every three years.

Growing habit Height 3–5 feet (1–1.5 m); herbaceous plant with fetid smell like old leather.

Flowering time June; small, tubular pale pink blossoms in dense terminal clusters.

Pest and disease prevention Usually free from pests and diseases; check occasionally.

Harvesting and storing Dig roots in fall or spring, before new shoots form; wash and dry quickly at 120°F (49°C) until brittle. Stores well. Prepare a soothing bath by adding a decoction made from valerian.

Special tips Cats and rats are attracted to the fetid smell of valerian, so use bunches of the plant to attract and catch them.

Other common names
Cat's valerian.

Precautions Don't take valerian for more than two weeks at a time.

SUITABLE SITES
The roots of valerian attract earthworms, so plant it in mixed borders and vegetable gardens. Because of its height, valerian is best suited to the back of the herb garden.

VERVAIN

Verbena officinalis Verbenaceae

This ancient perennial has a long religious and medicinal history and was sacred to many cultures. Today it is still used medicinally to treat tiredness, stress and minor cuts and bruises.

Best climate and site Zones 6–9. Prefers full sun.

Ideal soil conditions Ordinary, well-drained, chalky garden soil.

Growing guidelines Easily grows from seed sown outdoors; thin to 1 foot (30 cm). Take basal cuttings from established plants. Can self-sow. An organic mulch in spring will encourage better flowers and more foliage.

Growing habit Height 1–2 feet (30–60 cm); loosely branched with deeply lobed, oblong, sparsely located, slightly hairy leaves. Native to Europe, Western Asia and the Himalayas; naturalized in North America. Grows on roadsides, wastelands and in untended pastures.

Flowering time Summer to fall, small, tubular, pale lilac blossoms in spikes. No scent.

Pest and disease prevention Usually free from pests and diseases; check occasionally.

Harvesting and storing Foliage can be picked as required. If using the whole plant, harvest it when in bloom. The leaves and the whole plant can be dried; hang upside down in an airy, dry, warm place. Legend instructs that vervain should be harvested when neither Sun nor Moon is in the sky, and that pieces of honeycomb should be left in exchange.

Special tips A bath prepared with vervain soothes nervous exhaustion. Using two teaspoons of dried vervain for every cup of boiling water, make an infusion; allow it to steep for about 15 minutes. Rest a compress soaked in the infusion on closed eyelids for a few minutes to reduce swelling and refresh tired eyes; the infusion can also be used as an eye wash and as a hair tonic, massaged into the scalp and used in the final rinse. (A vervain preparation was one of the first commercially available hair products). A poultice made from the dried leaves will help to heal minor wounds.

Precautions May be toxic when taken internally. Studies have shown that vervain may depress the heart rate, constrict the bronchial passages and stimulate the intestines and the uterus.

Other common names
Simpler's joy, herb-of-the-cross, enchanter's herb.

Other species ❖ American vervain (*V. hastata*): Height 4–5 feet (1.2–1.5 m); blue flowers; also called blue vervain.

EASY GROWTH
Though vervain is classified as a perennial, it is short-lived. It does, however, self-sow and grows very easily when cultivated by seed. Its bushy habit makes it useful for filling empty spaces left by spring bulbs.

VIOLET, SWEET

Viola odorata Violaceae

Violets are early fragrant bloomers that grow well in shaded locations during cool weather. With its wonderful perfume and rich color, sweet violet is a delightful inclusion in any garden.

Best climate and site Zones 6–9. Partial shade.

Ideal soil conditions Any well-drained but moist garden soil.

Growing guidelines Sow seed shallowly outdoors in a cold frame as soon as ripe, or in fall; cover with burlap; thin to 1 foot (30 cm). Divide mature plants in fall, winter or early spring.

Growing habit Perennial; height 4–6 inches (10–15 cm); stemless, kidney-shaped, downy leaves.

Flowering time Spring; fragrant purple, violet, white or pink blossoms.

DESIGNER SCENT
When designing a garden for its fragrance, use sweet violets for a thick, scented ground cover under a bench or against a brick wall.

Grow sweet violets in pots for patios and decks. It doesn't grow well indoors.

Pest and disease prevention

Usually free from pests and diseases; check occasionally.

Harvesting and storing

Thoroughly dry flowers for culinary use; store in airtight containers. Petals may be added to fruit salads, flans and jams or candied and used to decorate cakes and desserts.

Other common names

Florist's violet.

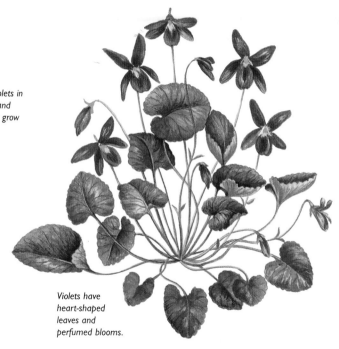

Violets have heart-shaped leaves and perfumed blooms.

WITCH HAZEL

Hamamelis virginiana Hamamelidaceae

Witch hazel is a hardy, small tree with scented yellow, fall flowers. Its forked branches were used as water divining rods and an extract from its bark has been a popular astringent for centuries.

Best climate and site Zones 5–9. Full sun to partial shade.

Ideal soil conditions Moist, rich garden soil.

Witch hazel toner cleans and refreshes skin.

Growing guidelines Store fresh seed in a warm room for five months, then at 40°F (4°C) for three months, before sowing. You can take cuttings or layerings from established plants.

Growing habit Height 8–15 feet (2.5–4.5 m); deciduous shrubs and small trees with smooth, gray to brown bark.

COMMERCIAL USE

When the young leaves, twigs and bark of the tree are commercially distilled for cosmetic products, the tannins are removed, leaving only the volatile oils.

Flowering time October to November; yellow threadlike petals followed by black nuts.

Pest and disease prevention
Usually free from pests and diseases; check occasionally.

Harvesting and storing
Collect leaves, twigs and bark as needed without damaging the tree. An infusion of the young, flower-bearing twigs can be used on a compress for bruises, sprains, muscle aches and insect bites; it can also be used as an astringent.

Other common names
American or Virginian witch hazel.

WINTER STUNNER
With its twisting stems, forking branches and threadlike petals, witch hazel makes a stunning impression in early winter, especially in the north where few plants bloom at that time.

WORMWOOD

Artemisia absinthium Compositae

Wormwood is a common member of sand-dune communities. The gray-green foliage and bushy growth make it an attractive garden plant. Try a wormwood spray on flea beetles and other pests.

Best climate and site Zones 6–9. Full sun to partial shade.

Ideal soil conditions Ordinary, well-drained soil.

Growing guidelines Sow seed shallowly outdoors in fall; or sow seed indoors in late winter, planting outdoors in late spring. Thin first-year plants to 15 inches (38 cm), then to 3 feet (90 cm) the second year. Divide established plants in early spring or early fall, take cuttings in late summer. Most plants last pyramidal seven years, with peak production during the second or third year.

BETTER ALONE
Wormwood is a pretty plant, despite its unappealing name. Use it in ornamental plantings or as an attractive, silvery hedge, but keep other plants away; few plants thrive when planted near wormwood.

Growing habit Height to 4 feet (1.2 m); hardy woody based perennial with gray-green finely dissected foliage.

Flowering time July to August; green-yellow in panicles.

Pest and disease prevention Wormwood is said to repel most insect and mammal pests.

Harvesting and storing Restrict harvests to the tops of plants when they flower after July. Hang in bunches to dry, then store in an airtight container. Withstands two harvests per season. Use in sachets to repel insects, or make a tea to repel aphids in the garden.

HEDGING HERB
Keep wormwood clipped back for dense growth; use the clippings for insecticidal and repellent sprays.

YARROW

Achillea millefolium Compositae

Yarrow displays light, delicate ferny foliage and long-lasting flowers. It is hardy and very easy to grow from seed and division. Plant in ornamental beds and the herb garden.

Biodynamic gardeners believe that yarrow increases the oil content of other aromatic herbs.

Best climate and site Zones 5–9. Full sun but shade tolerated.

Ideal soil conditions Ordinary, well-drained soil.

Growing guidelines Sow seed shallowly indoors in early spring, or outdoors in late spring. Divide large clumps in spring and fall to extend the planting. To promote flowering, pick blossoms often.

Growing habit Height to 3 feet (90 cm); a perennial with fernlike, finely divided, aromatic leaves that are rich in vitamins and minerals.

Flowering time June to September; numerous tiny white, pink or red florets in dense, flat clusters; has a pungent scent.

Pest and disease prevention Usually free from pests or diseases.

Harvesting and storing Pick flowers with plenty of stem and strip foliage before hanging in bunches to dry; holds color well. Use in dried arrangements and to make yellow or olive-colored dye.

Special tips Add a finely chopped leaf to a wheelbarrow load of compost to speed the process of decomposition.

Precautions May cause allergic reactions when taken internally.

Other common names Milfoil.

HOME FOR LADY BEETLES
Yarrow bears flat flower clusters that attract insects, including many beneficials. The ferny foliage provides good cover for lady beetles and other predaceous species. In the vegetable garden, deadhead vigilantly and use barriers to contain its growth.

PART THREE

USING HERBS

USING HERBS

HERB
CRAFT

Fragrances from the garden can lift the spirits or refresh the air, as well as evoking memories and recreating experiences long forgotten. Using herbs in your craft projects is a fun and practical way to get constant use out of your herbs. You can enjoy the aromas of herbs, whether sweet, spicy or pungent, all year round in the form of aromatic oils, potpourris, sachets and herbal arrangements. Express yourself creatively with herbs and invite your friends to share your enthusiasm. Pass around gifts of your own homemade herbal soaps and candles. For special gifts, arrange dried herbs into wreaths or baskets that smell as good as they look. Herbs are so versatile that you can surround yourself with herbal products every day of the year.

ESSENTIAL OILS

Essential oils are used in many kinds of herbal crafts. The scented oils you make from your own garden will have some of the same properties as professionally extracted essential oils, but not all. For this reason they may not be as effective in specific medicinal applications, but are very useful for potpourris, candles, soaps and perfumes.

Oil extracted from rose petals is used to add a floral note to herb craft.

Extracting with oil You can purchase essential oils in most craft and health food stores or prepare your own at home. If you plan to create your own essential oil, you'll need a lot of plant materials, since the amount of oil in most herbs is minute. Pack an enamel or glass pan with the herb or herbal blend of your choice, then cover with vegetable oil. Let it steep for at least a day, strain away the herbs and repeat the procedure using fresh herbs and the same oil. Follow this procedure five or more times. Store the oil in a tightly sealed glass bottle or jar. You can use the oil for making potpourris, candles or soaps.

Extracting with alcohol
Follow the same procedure as above, using undenatured ethyl

alcohol or vodka in place of the oil. Do not use rubbing alcohol. You can use these extracts for perfume bases.

Essentially yours To create a fragrance of your own, try combining oils. You can mix essential oils available in specialist shops, such as rose, citrus, jasmine, sweet woodruff, vanilla and sandalwood, with scents from your own garden. Your goal is to create a unique fragrance unlike any of the individual ingredients. As you experiment, make notes so that you may duplicate especially pleasing combinations.

Spice For a hint of the exotic, add finely ground spices to your scented oil. Make your own spice mix with equal parts of cinnamon, cloves, nutmeg and allspice. Or mix together equal parts of anise, cardamom and coriander.

Experimentation Essential oils can make a gift something very special. Use oils in papier-mâché to create scented beads and pendants. The strength of the aroma will depend on how much oil you use. You can add the oil to the flour and water base, to the newspaper itself, you could brush it onto the finished object before it is left to dry or you can add the oil to the paint you use to decorate the item. Try placing a drop of oil onto a bookmark and then sealing it in a plastic bag overnight so that the oil infuses the paper. Make a collection of beautifully shaped pieces of wood and sprinkle with your choice of oil. Any dried wood will soak up essential oils.

MAKING SCENTS
Lavender oil is easy to extract using the oil method and, unlike other homemade herbal oils, the scent is defined and strong.

POTPOURRI

Potpourris are long-lasting, fragrant mixtures of dried herbs and other crushed plant material. Making a potpourri preserves your favorite summer fragrances in a jar — just lift the lid and remember your garden's perfume.

Different combinations of dried herbs can create an aroma theme, such as woody, floral, culinary or citrus.

Making your own You may choose from recipes in herbal craft books or create your own custom blends at home using plants you've grown in your garden or purchased at herb shops or craft fairs. Either way, potpourris are simple to make from flowers and spice and everything nice. You will need a nonmetallic bowl, a wooden spoon, about 1 quart (1 L) of base material, several drops of essential oils and 1 tablespoon each of powdered spice and a fixative. The recipe can end there, or you can add other plant materials to modify the scent and appearance.

Base materials Rose petals, lavender flowers, pine needles, ground cedarwood, scented geranium leaves and other aromatic foliage or flowers in plentiful supply are good choices.

FIXING THE SCENT
Angelica seeds are a good fixative in potpourri.

To capture the essence of the culinary herb garden, use dried leaves, flowers and seedpods of basil, thyme or mint. Spread the clean materials on a screen and leave them to dry in a warm, dark, well-ventilated room for several days to two weeks. Stir the materials occasionally, for uniform drying. You may gather and dry base materials throughout the season, then store them in airtight containers until you are ready to use them. Just be sure that all ingredients are thoroughly dry.

Fixatives To preserve the fragrance of your potpourri, you will need to add a fixative to the base. Fixatives of animal origin, like ambergris, civet and musk, are expensive and hard to find. Plant-derived fixatives like orris root, vetiver root, rose attar, dried rosemary, sweet flag or tonka beans are less expensive and more readily available (usually from a pharmacist or craft store) and work just as well. Stir in 1 tablespoon of fixative for each quart (liter) of dried base.

Interesting extras Finally, add colorful plant materials of various shapes and textures for an interesting appearance. Include crushed or whole herb leaves like mint, basil, rosemary, lemon verbena or betony. Include whole or crumbled air-dried flowers like yarrow, statice or strawflowers. Add vanilla or tonka beans or other whole spices. To use orange or lemon peel, scrape away the white inner membrane before drying, then break the peel into tiny fragments that will dry quickly.

Enjoying your potpourri
Store your potpourri in tightly sealed jars in a dark, cool spot. Let it rest for at least one month before using it. Put it in ornamental jars or pots and open them for brief periods when you desire a hint of scent. To enhance the natural fragrance of your potpourri, add four drops of an aromatic oil.

HANDY HINT
For a more masculine scent, start your potpourri with a base of mint, pine or lemon balm.

HERB BAGS

Herb pillows and sachets make wonderful gifts and add something unique to your home. Choose fabrics and colors to match your furnishings or design a shape to fit in with a theme, such as a heart for Valentine's Day.

Herbal bath mitts, salts and infusions make a wonderful gift for people of all ages.

Herbal pillows

Hyssop helps you sleep.

Herb-scented pillows were originally a treatment for inducing sleep when stress prevented a restful night. It was thought that the fragrance of herbs such as hyssop would send you to sleep quickly. You can fill herbal pillows with whatever herbal blend suits you. Cut two pieces of fabric 8 inches (20 cm) square and stitch them, right sides together, along three sides. Turn them inside out and stuff the pocket loosely with potpourri or any mixture of dried herbs (without the stems), then stitch closed. Slip the pillow inside your pillowcase for a soothing sleep.

Herb sachets These fragrant sachets are great projects for children. Gather together squares of colorful cotton fabric cut in any shape or size; use pinking scissors along the edges for a pretty border. Place several tablespoons of crumbled potpourri in the center of each fabric square, gather together the edges and tie with a length of ribbon; you can also add lace and other special effects. Use sachets to scent drawers, closets, linen chests or luggage, or toss them in the tumble dryer to scent your clothing. When they begin to lose their scent, gather several in a glass jar and sprinkle them lightly with essential oils. Cover and let them sit for one week before reusing.

Herbal hotpads Set hot casserole dishes on these pads to release the fragrance of the herbs inside. Cut two 8-inch (20-cm) squares of prequilted fabric, place them with right sides together, then stitch them together on three sides. Turn inside out, then hem the open side. If you like, add

ADDING FRILLS
If you are a good sewer, you can add little extras like lace, frills and fine stitching to herb pillows.

press studs or buttons to fasten the open side. Make a second pillow of muslin, stuffing it loosely with a potpourri that suits your purpose before sealing. Slip the herbal pillow inside the open edge of the hotpad. You can refresh the scent with a few drops of essential oils.

> **THE LANGUAGE OF HERBS**
> The following herbs have meanings that may have originated from their traditional medicinal, or even magical, powers.
> **Aloe** healing
> **Angelica** inspiration
> **Basil** love or hate
> **Bay** victory, accomplishment, achievement
> **Bergamot** virtue
> **Borage** bravery
> **Dill** survival, good cheer
> **Chamomile** wisdom
> **Geranium, scented** happiness
> **Lavender** devotion
> **Marjoram** joy
> **Parsley** merriment
> **Rosemary** remembrance
> **Sage** long life, health
> **Southernwood** constancy
> **Tarragon** lasting involvement
> **Thyme** daring

HERBAL BATHING

Once you learn how simple it is to make your own scented soaps and bath oils, you'll want to make plenty to keep for yourself and to give as gifts. For the strongest aroma, use herbs like rosemary, lavender and thyme—their oils seem to linger on skin the longest.

Soft herbal soap

1½ cups dried herbs
1½ quarts (1.5 L) water
2 cups shredded
  pure soap
½ cup borax

In an enamel saucepan, combine the herbs and water and bring to a boil. Simmer for 30 minutes to release the oils. Reheat slowly and add the shredded soap and borax while stirring. Boil gently for three minutes, then cool. Pour the soft soap into covered containers.

Hard herbal soap

2 teaspoons dried herbs
  or 2 tablespoons fresh herbs
¼ cup water

SOOTHING SOAPS

Herbal bath products can soothe sore muscles and invigorate a tired mind.

Several drops essential oil
2 cups shredded
  pure soap

In an enamel saucepan, combine the herbs, water and oil and bring to a boil. Simmer for 30 minutes and then add the shredded soap, mixing thoroughly. Allow to cool for 15 minutes, then mix with your hands. Divide into six parts and roll each into a ball. Place the soaps on waxed paper to dry for several days.

Commercially produced herbal bath products.

Herbal baths

The soothing relaxation of herbal baths is hard to beat. Warm water slowly releases the fragrant oils that rise with the steam. For the most soothing bath, keep the water temperature around 96° to 98°F (35° to 36°C). A hotter bath will dry your skin and make you sleepy. To soften your skin, use chamomile or calendula blossoms, lemon balm leaves or marsh mallow root. The most relaxing herbal baths are made with catnip, hyssop, scented geranium or valerian root. To soothe dry skin, especially during cold weather, use a few drops of your own scented bath oil (see instructions below). Herbal bath bags are also wonderful

Bath oils

for massaging strained and tired muscles.

Herbal bath oil

½ teaspoon essential oil
½ cup sweet almond oil

Shake the ingredients together and store in a bottle away from light. Use just a small amount to massage weary muscles.

Herbal bath bag

½ cup dried herbs
  or 3 cups packed fresh herbs
8-inch (20-cm) square of muslin
  or cheesecloth

Center the herbs in the fabric, bring the edges together and secure tightly with string. To soften the water, you can add dried milk powder or a few teaspoons of oatmeal. Allow the bag to float in the water as the bath fills.

HERBAL INSECT REPELLENTS

Herbs were one of the first pest controls used by our earliest ancestors. Herbs work safely to control pests and they're easily recycled through the compost pile. Use herbs to help control pests on clothing and people with the following remedies.

Citrus works wonders in repelling all kinds of insect pests from the skin, clothes and air.

Insect repellent for clothing

½ cup cedar shavings
¼ cup each of at least four of: dried lemon verbena, lavender, pennyroyal, mint, rue, rosemary, santolina, southernwood, tansy or wormwood
2 tablespoons each of at least two of: whole cloves, cinnamon, nutmeg, lemon peel, peppercorns or bay leaves
5–10 drops essential oil of cedar, lemon, lavender or pine
2 tablespoons orris root

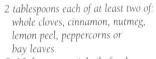

Bay leaves

Mix all of the ingredients together and allow the mixture to stand in a covered jar for one week. Cut scraps of fabric at least 8 inches

(20 cm) square. Place at least ½ cup of the mix in the center of the fabric, gather the edges together and tie securely with string or ribbon. You can hang the repellent sachets in closets or place them in stored luggage or linens to chase away the moths that like a meal of cotton or wool. Replace the sachets each season.

Insect repellent for skin

*1 teaspoon each of:
essential oils
of pennyroyal,
citronella,
eucalyptus, rosemary
and tansy
1 cup vegetable oil*

Rosemary

Shake ingredients together and store away from light. To repel outdoor insect pests, rub a small

amount between the palms of your hands, then apply to any exposed skin. Avoid applications to the face to prevent contact with your eyes. Reapply as necessary. If a rash develops, discontinue use.

Insect repellents for pets

Use one or both of the following herbal insect repellents for your pets, depending on the extent of the problem. You may also apply these repellents just as the flea season starts.

Herbal pet dip

*2 cups packed fresh peppermint,
pennyroyal or rosemary
1 quart (1 L) boiling water
4 quarts (4 L) warm water*

Prepare an infusion by pouring the boiling water over the herbs and allow it to steep for 30 minutes. Strain the liquid and dilute with the warm water. Saturate the

Pennyroyal

animal's coat thoroughly with the solution, allowing it to air-dry.

Herbal bedding Sew together small pillows of muslin or other cotton fabric. Stuff loosely with dried pennyroyal, cedar, rue, tansy, pine shavings or rosemary. Seal the bags and place in the folds of your pet's bedding. Refresh the dried materials weekly. Use at the first sign of flea activity.

HERBAL CANDLECRAFT

Herb Craft

Candles can help to create a refreshing or a
tranquil atmosphere and they are easy to make in
the home. Make them as strongly scented as you
like and leave in the plant materials—they will
add extra color and texture and make your
candle prettier and more interesting. You can use
any of the herbal scents you'd like to evoke
indoors. Lavender is a
favorite, along with
rosemary and
southernwood. Mix
your own blends
using materials
you've grown in
your herb garden.

CLEVER CANDLES
Float small herb candles in clear or
colored water and use as a dinner
table ornament. Herbal candles in
containers are perfect for outdoor
use on windy evenings.

Herb-scented candles
2 lb (1 kg) paraffin wax, broken into
  small pieces
2 cups dried herbs or 4 cups packed
  fresh herb leaves, blossoms or woody
  stems, or 1 fl oz (30 ml) essential oil
2 wax crayons or candle colorant
Sufficient candle wicking to reach the
  lengths of your candle molds
Several candle molds
  or recycled tin cans
Petroleum jelly
Pencils

Melt the wax in a bowl placed
over a saucepan of hot water,
then stir in the coloring.
Remove from heat and add the
plant materials or oil. Coat the
molds with petroleum jelly. Drop
a length of wicking to the bottom
of each mold, wrapping the
opposite end around a pencil
resting across the top of the mold

HANDY HINT

Paraffin wax comes in different melting points. The type of candle you are making will determine which melting point to buy. Paraffin is a petroleum by-product. It contains oil. The lower the melting temperature of the paraffin, the more oil content in the wax. You need low melt point wax for container candles and higher melt point wax for molded free-standing candles. Use the highest melt point wax for taper candles.

to keep the wick centered while you pour in wax. When the wax resembles a gel, pour it into the molds. Allow the candles to set overnight, then remove.

Decorating your candles
Instead of mixing the dried herbs into the wax, stick pressed herb flowers or leaves to the outside of a finished candle. Dip the plant material in melted wax that has had no color added and press it gently onto the surface of the candle. Holding the candle by the wick, dip the whole thing into the melted wax once or twice to form a seal over the flowers. The less colored the wax in the candle, the better the leaves and flowers will show through.

Herbal candle bases Using the instructions, make a paraffin candle. When it is completely dry, set it inside a mold that is a little bigger all the way around. Then sprinkle potpourri or dried herbs and flowers around the candle, over the base of the mold. Make a wax that has a higher melt point than the wax you used in your central candle. Pour this wax over the plant material in the base of the mold and allow it to dry.

Herbal candles offer variety of colors and scents.

SAY IT WITH HERBS

Miniature herbal bouquets were a special way of communicating long before the days of telephones, computers and facsimile machines. They're still a subtle way to get your message across. Tussie-mussies are composed of herbs and flowers with different meanings that vary from region to region. Since they were held to the nose to mask offensive odors in the days of poor sanitation, they were often called nosegays.

MESSAGE SCENT

Attach several lengths of narrow ribbon to your tussie-mussie and a card explaining the meaning of each plant. You can preserve the bouquet in silica gel, which absorbs moisture, or air-dry it and then sprinkle with fine orris root.

Tussie-mussies Select herbs and flowers that express your thoughts and pick them in the morning just after the dew has dried. Place the herb representing the most important sentiment in the center and surround it with sprigs or bunches of herbs that denote related thoughts in groups of three. Surround the tiny bouquet with fresh greens like geranium leaves or tansy, then secure the stems with a small rubber band. Cut an X in a doily and insert the stems, wrapping the doily to support the bouquet. You can place the arrangement in a vase with water. If your tussie-mussie will be traveling, wrap the stems with cotton soaked in water, then

PRETTY PURPLE
Violets are an attractive addition to herbal wreaths and arrangements. They combine well with lavender flowers.

with aluminum foil. You can preserve it in silica gel which absorbs moisture, or air-dry it and sprinkle it with fine orris root.

Herbal wreaths Wreaths are an attractive and fragrant way to display your own homegrown herbs and flowers. Start with a wreath frame of straw or wire and sufficient quantities of a dried or fresh base herb like southernwood or wormwood to cover the frame. Make small bunches of the base herb and wrap the cut end of each with florist's wire, then insert them into the frame or wrap them onto the frame with some florist's wire. Continue adding the base herb until the entire wreath form is covered. If you began with fresh material, hang the wreath to dry in a dark place for several weeks. You can attach contrasting herb bunches, dried flowers or ribbon-wrapped bundles of spices with more wire or use a glue gun. Create different themes to suit the occasion or mood. Store the wreath in a box between displays.

Dried herbal arrangements
1 wicker basket
Dried southernwood base material
Assorted dried herb bunches and flowers
Ribbons or bundles of spices

Pack the bottom of the basket with southernwood, then insert stems of herbs and flowers. Create contrast with silver and green foliage. Add ribbons or bundles of spices like cinnamon sticks or vanilla beans. Create a culinary arrangement for the kitchen. Fragrant arrangements will help to relieve the winter doldrums.

> **THE LANGUAGE OF FLOWERS**
>
> If you're making a tussie-mussie or a bouquet, use the following flowers to make them mean something really special.
> **Forget-me-not** true love
> **Goldenrod** encouragement
> **Iris** pure heart, courage, faith
> **Marigold** joy, remembrance
> **Rose** love, success
> **Violet** modesty, devotion
> **Yarrow** health
> **Zinnia** thoughts of absent friends

MEDICINAL HERBS

Compared with the precision of modern diagnosis and prescription medicine, herbal remedies can seem out of place and rather old-fashioned. Wild and homegrown herbal preparations were once the only medications used, but they've been largely replaced by synthetic drugs today. Modern physicians argue that synthetic medicines are superior since they are free of impurities, are of known strength and effects and are more stable. Herbal practitioners claim that when used properly, herbal remedies have an important role even today. In many countries, herbal remedies remain the only readily available treatment. And, of course, many of today's medicines are derived from naturally occurring plants.

THE HISTORY OF MEDICINAL HERBS

In most cultures around the world, the earliest forms of healing were based on herbs. People built up a wealth of knowledge based on experimentation within their environments and they handed that knowledge on to each generation. The arrival of written language provided us with records of the use of herbs as medicine as early as 3000 BC in Egypt, Babylon, China and India.

ARTFUL HEALING
Navajo healers used powdered rocks and herbs to create large pictures on the floor of a patient's dwelling. They believed the sandy grains could absorb evil sickness.

Herbs in the ancient world

Examples abound of the importance herbs played in the health and well-being of ancient peoples. In 600 BC, the philosopher and mathematician Pythagoras formed a center for higher learning which contained aromatic herb gardens designed to inspire the students' curiosity and generally invigorate them. In 300 BC, a medical school was set up in Alexandria where research was conducted into the uses of herbs in treating illness. This led to the creation of a document listing 600 herbs with

Ginseng root

a prescription for how to prepare them as a treatment for specific diseases. This book was considered the most important source of information on herbal medicine for the next 1,500 years.

Native American healers

Native Americans used many herbal medicines. From willow bark they extracted a pain-relieving ingredient, used in today's aspirin. Southeastern Cherokees believed every plant would cure a specific sickness. Iris roots ground with suet, lard and beeswax made an ointment for cuts and grazes. Juice of lady's slipper roots eased pain, soothed hysterics and relieved colds and flu.

Chinese herbs
Traditional Chinese medicine attaches a great deal of importance to the relationship of the human body with nature. Chinese people have

Star anise is used in many forms of healing.

been using natural herbs to treat a wide variety of diseases for over three thousand years. Herbal medicines are composed of roots, bark, flowers, seeds, fruits, leaves and branches. In China today there are over 3,000 different herbs that can be used for medical purposes. However, only 300 to 500 of these herbs are commonly used. It is important to use herbs grown in China rather than outside of their native environment and to use only Chinese herbs that have been prescribed by a professional.

HERBAL REMEDIES

Prepare herbal remedies, such as infusions, syrups, decoctions, compresses, poultices and ointments from your herb harvest to treat a number of common ailments. Refer to the Quick Guide to Medicinal Herbs on page 294 for the appropriate herb to use.

Herbal infusion

2 tablespoons dried herbs, or 1½ cups packed fresh herb leaves or flowers, washed and dried well
2 cups boiling water

Pour the boiling water over the herb, allowing it to brew for 15 minutes to several hours. Use a glass or ceramic pot and fresh spring, well or distilled water. Strain. Drink half to one cup of the infusion three to four times daily.

Herbal decoction

2 tablespooons dried herbs, or 1½ cups fresh bark, roots or stems, washed and dried well
2 cups boiling water

PURE FLAVOR
Brew herbal teas in a china, earthenware or glass pot.

HERBAL REMEDY PRECAUTIONS

Use all herbal remedies cautiously and
follow these guidelines:

❖ Always consult a doctor if you have
   painful or chronic symptoms.
❖ Don't mix herbal medicines with
   medical prescriptions.
❖ Always identify wild plants accurately
   and be aware of their properties
   and dangers.
❖ Check the "Plant by Plant Guide",
   starting on page 84, for poisonous
   herbs.
❖ Avoid large doses of any herb.
❖ Grow your own herbal medications
   for the best purity and quality, label

and store them and refresh the
supply each season.

❖ Follow the instructions for harvesting
   and storing herbs properly.
❖ Stop using any herbal medicine if
   you notice any side effects, such
   as headaches, dizziness or an
   upset stomach.
❖ Avoid using herbal medicines if you
   are pregnant or nursing, unless you
   have the consent and supervision of
   an obstetrician.
❖ Do not give herbal medicines to
   children less than two years old
   without the consent of your doctor.

Add the herbs to boiling water in an enamel saucepan, then simmer gently, without boiling, for 30 minutes. Strain and drink half to one cup three to four times daily.

Herb teas The difference between an infusion and a tea is the length of time the herbs are allowed to steep in the water. Herb tea should be lightly colored and mild. Steep for only 5 to 10 minutes for the best flavor. A strong tea will be bitter and might cause unexpected side effects if the herb has medicinal properties. Herb teas don't have to be medicinal for you to enjoy them. After a stressful day, a soothing cup of herbal tea is relaxing and satisfying. Use ½ to 1 teaspoon fresh herb leaves for each cup of boiling water, and make herbal tea by pouring boiling water over the herb in a clean china or glass pot. (Metals can change the flavor of some herbs.)

Peppermint tea is highly refreshing.

HERBAL REMEDIES continued

Herbal compress Follow the instructions for preparing an infusion or decoction, then soak a towel in the warm liquid. Wring it out and lay it upon the affected area, covering it with a dry towel. As the compress cools, replace it with a warm one. Continue treatment for 30 minutes or until the skin is flushed or tingly. A hot compress made with mustard, cayenne, garlic or ginger will improve circulation and is good for treating nasal and chest congestion. Compresses prepared with herbs like comfrey or aloe are good for sprains and bruises.

Garlic

Herbal poultice
¼ cup dried herbs or 3 cups fresh herbs, washed, dried and minced
4 cups oatmeal

Mix the herbs and oatmeal with enough hot water to form a paste. Place the paste directly on the skin and cover with a towel. As it cools, replace it with a warm one. Continue treatment for 30 minutes. Don't use hot, spicy herbs like mustard that may burn the skin. Poultices are used to draw out infection and relieve muscle aches.

Herbal plaster Place dried or fresh herbs or a freshly mixed paste (see the poultice recipe above) in the folds of a light towel or muslin, then lay the plaster on injured area. Since the herbs don't have direct contact with the skin,

QUICK RELIEF
Herbal plasters are handy for immediate relief of minor injuries.

plasters are useful for particularly sensitive wounds like minor burns; flush with water and then apply a plaster of echinacea paste. Plus, because there is no direct contact, you can use hot herbs like red pepper which can relieve muscle and joint pain.

Herbal oil

¼ cup dried herbs or 3 cups fresh
   herbs, washed and dried well
2 cups cold pressed olive oil or
   vegetable oil

Crush the herbs and add the oil.
Let steep for several days; strain,
then bottle.

Herbal ointment

1–1½ oz (30–45 g) melted
   beeswax or rendered lard
Herbal oil

Mix together the liquid
beeswax or lard and herbal
oil. Store in a cool, dry
place for one week.

Herbal syrup

¼ cup dried herbs or 3 cups
   packed fresh herbs, washed
   and dried well
1 quart (1 L) water
1–2 tablespoons honey

Combine the ingredients in an
enamel saucepan. Bring to the boil
and continue at a slow boil until
the liquid is reduced by half. Add
the honey and store refrigerated
for up to one month. Garlic is
commonly used in a syrup for
antibiotic and antiseptic
applications.

Herbal tincture

¾ cup powdered dried herb
2 cups brandy, vodka or gin

Mix together ingredients in
a glass bottle and allow to
steep, shaking occasionally, for
several weeks.

*As well as being delicious,
honey is used as a base
in medicinal herbal syrup.
Also, because of its healing
properties, beeswax is
used with herbal oils in
external ointments.*

THERAPEUTIC HERBAL OILS

For effective therapy, only pure essential oils should be used. These are the essences that have been extracted by steam distillation, solvent extraction, expression, maceration or enfleurage. Reconstituted products or chemical copies do not have the necessary medicinal properties.

HANDY HINT
Pure essential oils when dropped on blotting paper will impregnate it, then evaporate and disperse, without leaving any kind of oily patch.
A product containing vegetable oil will leave an oily mark.

BUYING PURE
When buying products containing essential oils, go to health shops rather than shops that sell cosmetics.

oil dispersant

carrier oils

base cream

essential oils

Base oils Because they are so powerful, essential oils are usually diluted by mixing with a less powerful oil, called a base or carrier oil, before being used directly on the skin. The most popular base oils are almond for body massage, apricot and jojoba for younger facial skin and wheatgerm and avocado for mature, dry facial skin. Depending on the essential oil you're using, one drop may be all you need; the base oil will spread its therapeutic and aromatic properties over the area of the body you want to treat.

Using oils Most commercially prepared essential oils will have directions for use on the bottle. In general, use two to three drops in a bowl of hot water to inhale the oil's vapor; for body massage use five drops for each teaspoon of base oil; in baths use eight drops of essential oil.

BASICS FOR HOME CARE

There are hundreds of essential oils to choose from, but a basic few, kept on hand, will do for therapeutic use.

Lavender According to herbalists, lavender oil should grace every home. It is a natural antibiotic, antiseptic, anti-depressant and sedative, and helps the healing process in burns and scalds.

Peppermint Peppermint should not be used during pregnancy, but at all other times it is very useful in digestive disorders, as well as stimulating the respiratory system. As an inhalant, peppermint will provide temporary relief of sinusitis, bronchial cough and the symptoms of colds and flu. A few drops in a carrier oil can be massaged onto the stomach area, in a clockwise direction, to relieve nausea.

Chamomile This oil is helpful in treating anxiety, but it should never be used by people with low blood pressure. There are a few different types of chamomile oil, the most beneficial of

which are German and Roman. Both of these types can be used mixed in jojoba oil as a massage on the forehead and temples to soothe the effects of headaches, insomnia, nervous tension and stress. This same mix can be used on acne, boils and mild burns.

Geranium This oil is said to work mostly on the emotions. It is not extracted from the common, brightly colored geranium, but from the species *Pelargonium* which is also known as lemon plant. You can use geranium, mixed with a massage oil, to treat acne, dermatitis, bruises and eczema.

Rosemary Rosemary stimulates both the body and the mind, so it is particularly good to use in the morning. For the temporary relief of headaches and muscular pain, to assist peripheral circulation and to relieve eczema, insomnia and tension, use rosemary in the bath, in a vaporizer or in a massage oil. To treat dandruff, massage a few drops of rosemary into the scalp.

AROMATHERAPY

Aromatherapy is the use of natural plant essences (essential oils) in healing, relaxation and stress. Aromatherapy is literally "therapy by smell." The fragrant natural essential oils of herbs and flowers have a beneficial effect on the body.

How it all works Each herb releases different scent molecules which are detected by the olfactory nerves in the nose. These nerves are directly linked with the areas of the brain that deal with emotions, memory and creativity. The messages picked up these nerves travel quickly to the brain and can have an immediate effect on particular chemicals being injected into the body; in turn this can affect the workings of bodily functions. The job of an

MIXING OIL AND WATER

Diffusers are especially made to heat essential oils in order to release their aroma. A few drops of the oil are added to water in a bowl; the bowl is then heated from below. When buying oils labeled "aromatherapy," check whether it is an essential oil mixed in a base oil. If so, it is meant for massage.

aromatherapist is to work out how the body can benefit from this chemical reaction to scents. Since the aroma of a plant is contained in its oil, extracting the oil produces a very concentrated scent that should be used carefully. Of course the effects of a herb's aroma can be enjoyed just by smelling the plant itself.

Combinations of oils By mixing two or more essential oils, you can create an aroma that has added therapeutic properties. It is important, however, to get the ratio right. You will need to refer to a specialist publication or a professional for recommended quantities and combinations.

Heating the oil Vaporization is the easiest method of releasing the aroma of essential oils; the aroma is then absorbed by the body through inhalation. The idea

---

HANDY HINT

You can release the aroma of essential oils many ways. Try adding essential oils to the water in a humidifer. Place one drop on a log at least half an hour before you put it in the fire. Touch a cold light globe with a drop of essential oil before putting it into the light socket.

---

behind this process is that heating the oils allows their molecules to be released into the air.
Inhalation: Add six drops of the selected essential oil to four cups of steaming water in a bowl or sink. Cover your head with a towel and lean over the bowl with your face well away, keeping your eyes closed. Breathe deeply through your nose for about one minute. This is particularly helpful if you have a cold or cough.
Vaporizers, or diffusers: These are made for use with essential oils. Some are heated by the flame

of a candle, others by electricity. It's important that the bowl isn't porous so it can be cleaned and used for a different oil; otherwise you may be mixing scents.

Stove-top simmers Here is yet another way to enjoy the aroma of your garden herbs. These mixtures are especially good if you plan to spend the day in the kitchen. Just set them in a saucepan toward the back of the stove where the gentle heat will release the oils. Add ½ cup dried herbs to 2 cups of water. Keep an eye on the mixture to make sure all of the water doesn't simmer away, or the herbs may burn. To create a spicier scent, mix your herbs with equal parts of allspice, star anise, cinnamon sticks, ginger root, whole cloves and citrus peel. You can also add a drop or two of commercially produced essential oils to accent the aroma.

QUICK GUIDE TO MEDICINAL HERBS

Use the following as a quick reference to some of the more common and beneficial medicinal herbs and their soothing and healing properties.

Aloe Apply the fresh transparent gel from the leaves externally to scalds and sunburn, blisters, scrapes and acne to promote healing and prevent infection. First clean the wound properly. Then cut off a few inches (centimeters) of one of the lower, older, leaves of the plant. Slice it lengthwise and you'll see the clear gel start to exude. Rub it gently on the wound. The remaining section of leaf on the plant will heal itself quickly and can be used again. Do not take aloe internally.

Aloe

Arnica Make a tincture from the flower heads and apply as a compress to soothe sore muscles and sprains. Do not take this herb internally.

Barberry Prepare a decoction by boiling ½ teaspoon of the dried, powdered roots in 1 cup of water for 15 to 30 minutes a day. Drink up to one cup a day before meals for relief of infections and constipation.

Chamomile

Calendula Make a compress from the flowers and apply to stings, bruises, scrapes and burns.

Catmint

Catmint Catmint has a calming effect on the muscles of the digestive tract and aids digestion. Make an infusion using two teaspoons of the dried flowers and leaves per cup of boiling water; let it steep for 15 minutes. Drink up to three cups a day.

Chamomile Like catmint, chamomile will relieve cramps and upset stomachs and aid digestion. It also helps heal stomach ulcers, relieves arthritic joint inflammation, helps to prevent infection in wounds and can stimulate the immune system. Make an infusion from the flowers and drink one cup two to three times daily.

Comfrey Make a compress or poultice from the fresh leaves and apply to bruises and sprains. Or make an ointment to treat minor burns, scalds and abrasions.

Dandelion Make an infusion from the leaves or a decoction from the roots. Drink one cup up to three times daily as a diuretic, digestive aid and laxative.

Dandelion

Eucalyptus Make an infusion from the leaves and inhale the vapors as a decongestant and to relieve other cold and flu symptoms. For its antibacterial properties, crush and rub the leaves (or a drop of eucalyptus essential oil) into minor cuts after they have been thoroughly cleaned.

Eucalyptus

Fennel Make an infusion from the dried seeds or fresh leaves and drink one cup up to three times daily to soothe an upset stomach and to relieve flatulence.

Garlic Use raw cloves to prepare antibiotic and antiseptic infusions, syrups and plasters. Garlic also reduces blood sugar levels, may help to eliminate lead and other toxic heavy metals from the body.

(If you ingest raw garlic, chew a sprig of parsley afterward to freshen your breath.)

Hops Make an infusion from the fresh "cones" and drink one cup up to three times daily to calm nerves, prevent infection and settle an upset stomach. For insomnia, use dried, aged hops in an infusion.

Horehound Horehound contains chemicals which can loosen phlegm. Make an infusion from the leaves and drink one cup up to three times daily as an expectorant. Make a syrup from the leaves and take ½–1 teaspoon up to three times daily for coughs, colds, sore throats and bronchitis.

Horehound

Hyssop Make an infusion from the leaves and tops and drink up to two cups per day as a cold and flu remedy. Add honey to disguise hyssop's bitter taste. A compress of hyssop may inhibit the growth of cold sores; use 1 ounce (30 g) of dried hyssop leaves and flowers per pint (600 ml) of boiling water. Steep for 20 minutes and cool. Soak a clean, soft piece of cloth in the infusion and apply to any areas showing signs of herpes simplex virus.

Hyssop

Marsh Mallow A spongy substance in marsh mallow roots, called mucilage, swells to form a gel when it comes in contact with water. Use the gel to soothe cuts, scrapes and minor burns. Make a decoction from the roots and drink one cup up to three times daily to soothe sore throats and calm upset stomachs.

Parsley Parsley's volatile oil is contained in all parts of the plant, but is most concentrated in the seeds. Make an infusion from the leaves or seeds and drink one cup two to three times daily as a diuretic and mild laxative. Parsely also has some antihistamine properties, which may make it helpful in

Parsley

reducing the effects of allergies. To freshen breath, chew a few sprigs.

Passionflower
Passionflower tea can have a tranquilizing effect on the central nervous system. Make an infusion from the dried leaves and drink one cup up to three times daily to relieve nervous tension, aid digestion and ease menstrual discomfort. For first aid in the garden, crush a few passionflower leaves and flowers and rub them on minor cuts as you make your way to properly cleaning the wounds.

Passionflower

Peppermint Peppermint oil is mostly menthol which helps to smooth the muscle lining of the digestive tract and act as an antispasmodic. It may smooth other muscles too, such as the uterus, which is why pregnant women should be cautious using peppermint products. For everyone else, peppermint is wonderful as a decongestant or for an upset stomach. Make an infusion from the leaves and drink one cup up to three times daily. A few drops of the essential oil on minor wounds and burns may help to anesthetize pain and prevent infection. Use it in herbal sachets for a refreshing bath.

Rose The fragrant petals of the rose will perfume the air and help to cover up unwanted smells, but it is the hips, or fruit, of the plant that is used medicinally. Rosehips

Rose

are high in vitamin C when fresh; drying can destroy up to 90 percent of the vitamin content. To treat cold and flu symptoms, make an infusion from the hips and drink one cup up to three times daily.

Rosemary Make an infusion from the leaves and flowers and drink up to three cups daily as an antiseptic or for stomach upsets. Use the infusion as a rinse after shampooing and conditioning hair.

Rosemary

Sage Use the crushed, fresh leaves as a preliminary antiseptic on minor wounds in the garden. Make an infusion from the leaves and drink as needed, up to three cups daily, for cold symptoms and stomach upsets and to aid digestion. An infusion of sage may also reduce perspiration.

Thyme Make an infusion from the leaves and stems and drink up to three cups daily for cold, flu and allergy symptoms.

Valerian Make an infusion from the roots and drink about half a cup once or twice daily to calm the nerves and relieve insomnia, headaches, stress and menstrual tension and discomfort.

Witch Hazel Make a decoction from the leaves or bark and use it as a compress for skin problems, aching joints, sore muscles, cuts, bruises and insect bites.

Yarrow Make an infusion from the flowers and leaves and drink one cup, warmed, to up to three times daily for indigestion.

Yarrow

USING HERBS

HERBS
IN THE
KITCHEN

Herbs are a welcome addition to any kitchen. Your own herb garden, brimming with herbs that are useful for garnish, like parsley and chives, and herbs that are important for flavor and aroma, like basil and rosemary, lets you add a special touch to all your dishes. A pantry well stocked with special herbal treats will also enable you to have what you need for that extra something. Sprinkle herbal vinegars and oils on salads all year round for a quick alternative to bottled dressing. Herbal jellies and honeys are simple to prepare and can be used in a surprising number of ways, as well as making ideal gifts. And don't overlook the delights of candied flowers—these delicacies will last for months.

COOKING WITH HERBS

If you want to learn how to use the culinary herbs, grow them! A bushy, fragrant herb plant just outside the kitchen door is the best inspiration for culinary success. If you've never used herbs before, start by following simple recipes that appeal to you.

A LOT FROM A LITTLE

Growing just a few of the classics can give you endless culinary options. Bunch herbs together for a bouquet garni you can use in soups, stews and sauces. Or grind them into a paste using a mortar and pestle.

Experimenting with recipes

Most cookbooks offer a variety of dishes that require herbs for flavoring. Another way to become familiar with herbs is to add them to foods you already make. Add snips of fresh herbs to scrambled eggs or omelettes, trying a new herb each time. Or add them to bland foods like cottage cheese, cream cheese or rice. Once you've developed preferences for certain herbs, try combining them with others in the same foods.

How much to use When using herbs, a little bit goes a long way. Culinary herbs should be used sparingly, to enhance the natural flavors of other ingredients in the recipes. Most herbs should be added at the end of the recipe. Their flavors are released with

gentle heat, but are lost if cooked for longer than 30 minutes. An exception is bay leaf, which stands up to a long stewing time.

Releasing the flavor When using fresh herbs in recipes, save the leaves, flowers, or seeds and discard the stems. Snip the leaves with kitchen shears, or if you need larger quantities, bunch the leaves on a cutting board and mince the pile with a sharp knife. Food processors are useful for chopping large batches of herbs for recipes like pesto or tabbouleh. Many cooks rub fresh and dried herbs between their hands before adding them to the pot, in order to crush the herbs and release their essential oils. If your recipe calls for a fine powder, grind dried herbs with a pestle and mortar, or purchase a special spice grinder. A coffee grinder works well, but be sure to carefully wipe it clean after

use. Ground herbs should be used immediately for the best flavor. You can freeze the leftovers in airtight containers. Remember, though, that it's very important to wash and dry herbs thoroughly before using them in the kitchen.

Using fresh herbs You can substitute fresh for dried herbs in most recipes. Since fresh herbs contain more water than dried ones, use two to three times more fresh herbs than the dried measurement to get the same amount of essential oil. Fresh herbs are great salad additions. Add chopped or whole sprigs of basil, chervil, chives, dill, oregano, thyme, tarragon or whatever flavors or blends you enjoy. Use herb blossoms from chives, borage and nasturtium to garnish the finished salad. Or use fresh herb leaves like nasturtiums as a wrapping for pâté.

A CLEAN BREAK
A sharp knife is a must in the kitchen, and is especially important when chopping herbs so that the leaves and stems mince rather than tear.

HERB BUTTERS

Herb butters are colorful and fragrant spreads for warm biscuits, vegetables, poultry, fish or meat. Add a dab to pasta or rice, or use a herb butter to baste grilled or baked fish. Make it up when your herbs are plentiful and use it when needed.

Basic butters Most herb butter recipes call for unsalted butter. For less cholesterol, substitute margarine. Let it soften at room temperature, then beat in the herbs and other seasonings by hand or with an electric mixer. For the best flavor, chill for at least three hours before serving. Pack the flavored butter into molds or basins; form balls with a melon-baller; or shave curls from chilled butter with a sharp knife. Store it wrapped tightly in plastic for up to one month in the

Fresh chives

TASTY SPREAD
Spread herb butter on fresh, crusty bread for a tasty treat. Or use it to baste fish and poultry.

refrigerator, or keep frozen for up to three months. Create your own herb butter to suit your menu or follow the recipes here.

Basic rules Remember to wash the herbs carefully before using them; soil and grit can hide in the small folds of leaves. Dry them thoroughly because even small amounts of water will affect the texture of the butter. For 1 tablespoon of fresh herbs, you may substitute 1½ teaspoons of dried herbs or, if you prefer, ½ teaspoon of seeds.

Simple herb butter

1 tablespoon minced fresh herbs, washed and dried well
4 oz (125 g) butter, softened

Mix ingredients together. Use herbs singly or in combinations. Try mint with dill, dill with garlic, chives with lovage or marjoram.

Parsley butter

⅓ cup minced, fresh, thoroughly washed, curled parsley
1 tablespoon lemon juice
1 teaspoon Worcestershire sauce
8 oz (250 g) unsalted butter or margarine, softened

Garlic butter

4–6 cloves garlic, finely minced
8 oz (250 g) unsalted butter or margarine, softened

Garlic and lemon butter

2 teaspoons minced fresh garlic (don't use pre-minced garlic)
2 tablespoons lemon juice
4 oz (125 g) unsalted butter or margarine, softened

Mixed herb butter I

1 teaspoon each minced fresh marjoram, thyme and rosemary
¼ teaspoon each minced fresh garlic, basil and sage
4 oz (125 g) butter, softened

Keep plenty of garlic on hand for herb butters.

Mixed herb butter 2

½ cup each minced fresh parsley and lovage
1½ teaspoons minced fresh thyme
½ teaspoon each minced fresh sage, marjoram and garlic
¼ teaspoon freshly ground pepper
8 oz (250 g) butter, softened

Mix all ingredients together. Mixed herb butters are particularly good for poultry stuffings.

HERBAL VINEGARS

Try combining several herbs to create your own special vinegars. Garlic and chives combine well with most of the strongly flavored herbs, such as basil, dill and thyme. Mix equal parts of parsley, thyme and rosemary for a special blend.

Basic herbal vinegar

1–2 cups packed fresh herbs, washed and dried well or 2–3 tablespoons herb seeds, or 10 cloves garlic
4 cups vinegar (5 percent acidity)

Wash and dry the herbs (any leftover water will turn the vinegar cloudy), then pack them into hot, sterilized glass jars using a wooden spoon. Fill with vinegar, leaving 1 inch (2.5 cm) at the top. With the spoon, push the herbs down and lightly bruise them. If you're using seeds or garlic, first bruise them gently using a pestle and mortar. Cover the tops of the jars with tightly placed cling plastic before putting on the metal lids to prevent chemical reactions between the vinegar and metal, then screw the seal tight. Let the herbs steep in a warm, dark place (such as a cupboard near the stove or a shelf near the fireplace) for three to six weeks, then strain the flavored vinegar through a paper coffee filter. Pour the clear vinegar into hot, sterilized jars or decorative bottles, add a few sprigs of fresh herbs and cap.

Wine-based vinegars

Wine-based vinegars are ideal as a base for herbal vinegars, since their flavor is mild and blends well with the herbs. Use white-wine vinegar with chive blossoms, lavender, marjoram, nasturtium flowers and leaves, dark opal and lemon basil, tarragon and thyme. Use

MAKING GIFTS

As well as experimenting with combinations of herbs in your vinegars, use bottles with different shapes and sizes, and try unusual seals for special homemade gifts.

red-wine vinegar with bay leaves, dill, fennel, garlic, lovage, mint, sweet basil and thyme.

Storing herbal vinegar Once your herb vinegar has aged, transfer it to decorative bottles that

you can buy from cooking-supply stores or through catalogues. Or use recycled bottles from salad dressing, ketchup, sauce and wine.

Sealing the bottles For a special effect, seal the bottle caps

with scented wax. Melt 1 cup of paraffin with ¼ cup of mixed spices (try cinnamon, nutmeg, cloves or allspice) in a tall can placed in 1 inch (2.5 cm) of water in a saucepan. Melt the mixture slowly (paraffin ignites easily). Make sure your vinegar bottles are capped tightly, then turn them over and dip the top of each bottle (just past the cap) into the melted wax. Dip them several times, allowing the wax to dry (less than 30 seconds) between dips. Add more wax and spices as needed. You can store any leftover wax in the same can. Let the bottles cool before handling them. To open, lightly score the wax just under the end of the cap.

HERB-FLAVORED OILS & DRESSINGS

Herbs in the Kitchen

You can use flavored oils wherever a recipe calls for oil in sauces and marinades, or wherever you want an extra touch of flavor. Homemade salad dressings are far superior to the commercial versions. Make them yourself and cut the oil in half to limit calories. Use any single herb or combination that suits your menu.

Tarragon

Herbal oil

¼ cup packed fresh herbs, washed and dried well, or 3 cloves garlic
1 cup olive or vegetable oil

Place the herbs in the bottom of a hot, sterilized jar. Heat the oil in a saucepan until just warm, then pour it into the jar. Let the flavored oil cool, then cover tightly and store in the refrigerator. Use garlic oil in Chinese stir-fries. Rosemary oil is delicious rubbed on lamb before grilling or barbecuing. Basil oil is excellent with fresh or cooked tomatoes and can be used as a sauce for pasta. Dill oil gives flavor to hot, boiled potatoes. Use oregano oil to marinate black olives.

Basil gives oil a rich flavor. Try it on pasta.

French dressing

2 tablespoons minced fresh herbs, washed and dried well
¾ cup olive oil
¼ cup vinegar

Shake all ingredients together.

Herb and yogurt dressing

2 tablespoons minced fresh herbs, washed and dried well
1 cup plain yogurt

Shake all ingredients together.

Dried herb dressing

1 cup dried parsley
½ cup each dried basil, thyme, savory and marjoram
¾ cup olive oil
¼ cup vinegar

Mix together the dry ingredients and store in an airtight container.

Each time you need a dressing, shake together one tablespoon of the dry herb mix with the oil and vinegar.

Salting herbs Herb salt can add instant flavor to your oils and dressings and encourage you to reduce actual salt use.

Herb salt for the table

1 cup non-iodized sea salt or kosher salt

1 cup packed fresh herbs, washed, dried and minced, or 2 tablespoons dried herbs (basil, chives, garlic, marjoram, oregano, rosemary, savory, tarragon and thyme work especially well.)

MAIN ATTRACTION

Flavorsome herbal oils add interest to salads, sauces and marinades. As well as being a handy ingredient, they can be a main attraction when used straight from the bottle.

Grind the salt and herbs together in a blender, or finely crumble the herbs by hand and mix them into the salt. Store in an airtight jar or place the mixture in a shaker, and use it to add flavor to your meals. You can make different mixtures to accompany vegetables or meat.

HERBAL SWEETS

Herbal sweets are simple to prepare and make attractive and useful gifts. Surprise your family and friends with jars of herb-flavored honeys they can use in tea, baskets of candied flowers they can nibble on and pots of herbal jellies they can spread on toast.

Herb-flavored honeys Use herb-flavored honey instead of sugar in drinks and recipes or combine it with an equal part of butter for a sweet spread. Use any herb singly or combine a few. Good herbs to use include anise seed, coriander, fennel seed, lavender, sage, lemon verbena, thyme, marjoram, mint, rose-scented geranium and rosemary.

Herbal honey
1 tablespoon fresh herbs, washed and dried well or 1½ teaspoons dried herbs, or ½ teaspoon herb seeds
2 cups honey

EXTENDED SEASON
Edible blossoms are a treat normally limited to the growing season, but preserved with sugar and stored properly, they'll last up to six months. Try rose petals and lavender flowers.

Bruise the herbs lightly and place them in a muslin bag or directly into a saucepan. Pour the honey into the pan and heat until just warm; high heat will spoil it. Pour into hot, sterilized, glass jars and seal. Store at room temperature for a week, then rewarm the honey and strain out the herbs. Return the honey to hot, sterilized jars and seal. You can leave the herbs in for texture and color.

Making candied flowers Pick the blossoms just after they've opened; leave enough stem attached to hold as you work.

Candied herb blossoms
1 egg white, beaten until frothy
Fresh blossoms, washed and drained
Caster sugar

Beat the egg white until it is frothy. Using a soft brush, thoroughly coat the petals with the egg white and sprinkle all surfaces with sugar. Place on waxed paper and dry in a warm place for two days. Store in a tightly sealed glass jar.

Herbal jellies Use herbal jellies just like fruit jellies or use to glaze roast or grilled meat, fish and chicken. Good herbs to use are mint, tarragon and rosemary.

Apple and mint jelly
4½ pounds (2.25 kg) apples, washed
honey, water and fresh mint leaves

Quarter the fruit, but don't pare or core it. Place in a pot and add water to half cover. Cook over low heat until soft (about one hour). Place the fruit in a jelly bag and drain out the liquid. (Squeezing the bag will make a cloudy jelly.) Measure the juice and add ½ cup of honey for every 1 cup of juice. Boil until syrupy. To test, put a spoonful on a cold plate and chill in the freezer for a few minutes. If it gels, it's done. If not, keep cooking and try again. Just before removing the jelly from the heat, stir in ¼ cup packed mint leaves for every quart (liter) of juice. Strain and ladle into hot, sterilized jars. Seal the jars tightly.

PROPER STORAGE
Store candied blossoms in a tightly sealed glass jar with wax paper between layers.

PLANT HARDINESS ZONE MAP

A hardiness zone map enables you to match the climate where you live with herbs that will thrive there—the key to success in a herb garden.

Using the map Plants grow best within an optimum range of temperatures. The range may be wide for some species and narrow for others. Plants also differ in their ability to survive frost and in their sun or shade requirements. This map of the United States and Canada is divided into 10 zones. Each zone is based on a 10°F (5.6°C) difference in average annual minimum temperature. Some areas are considered too high in elevation for plant cultivation and so are not assigned to any zone. There are also island zones that are warmer or cooler than surrounding areas because of differences in elevation; they have been given a zone different from the surrounding areas. Many large urban areas are in a warmer zone than the surrounding land. The zone ratings indicate conditions where designated plants will grow well and not merely survive. Many plants may survive in zones warmer or colder than their recommended zone range. Remember that other factors, including wind, soil type, soil moisture, humidity, snow and winter sunshine may have a great effect on growth. When buying a herb, have a look at the zone information listed on its tag, or refer to the guide in this book.

Zone 1	Below -50°F (Below -45°C)
Zone 2	-50° to -40°F (-45° to -40°C)
Zone 3	-40° to -30°F (-40° to -34°C)
Zone 4	-30° to -20°F (-34° to -29°C)
Zone 5	-20° to -10°F (-29° to -23°C)
Zone 6	-10° to 0°F (-23° to -18°C)
Zone 7	0° to 10°F (-18° to -12°C)
Zone 8	10° to 20°F (-12° to -7°C)
Zone 9	20° to 30°F (-7° to -1°C)
Zone 10	30° to 40°F (-1° to 4°C)

Canada

Pacific
Ocean

United States
of America

Atlantic
Ocean

FIRST PORT OF CALL
It's important to choose herbs that
grow well in your area. The Plant
Hardiness Zone Map is your first port
of call when deciding what herbs to
buy. Then other considerations can
come into play, such as the
microclimate of your yard.

GLOSSARY

Glossary

annual A plant that has a life span of one year or less.

biennial A plant that has a life span of two years.

Dandelion

bouquet garni A bunch of herbs, most commonly including a bay leaf, thyme and parsley or chervil tied together with string, or in a muslin bag. It is used in the cooking of soups, stews and sauces and removed before serving. The essential oils of the herbs provide a subtle flavor and aroma.

compress A pad of soft material moistened with a warm herbal infusion or decoction and placed on a wound for medicinal purposes.

cutting A section taken from the stem of a plant in order to reproduce the plant. Most herbs are easily propagated from cuttings.

decoction An extract of a herb made by simmering the roots and bark of a plant (most commonly dried) in water.

division The propagation of a plant by removing a section from the root and replanting it.

fines herbes A mixture of minced fresh herbs, such as basil, chervil, chives, marjoram, tarragon and thyme, stirred into foods at the end of cooking to add color as well as flavor.

fixative A substance that is added to the base of potpourri to preserve the fragrance. Fixatives

can be of animal origin, such as ambergris, civet and musk, or derived from plants, such as orris root, vetiver root, rose attar, dried rosemary, sweet flag or tonka beans. One tablespoon of fixative is used for each quart (liter) of dried base.

infusion The extract of an herb made by steeping or soaking the flowers, leaves and stems of the plant in boiling water.

layering The propagation of a plant by means of burying one of its still-attached, long, flexible stems into the soil next to the plant.

Hyssop

marinade A liquid in which foods are soaked in order to tenderize and flavor them. Commonly meat or poultry is soaked in a marinade containing wine, vinegar and herbs for several hours or overnight.

Lavender

mulch A material that is used to cover the surface of your garden soil in order to keep the soil warmer in winter and cooler in summer, to retain moisture and to hinder the growth of weeds. Mulch can be an organic material, such as compost, grass clippings or shredded leaves, or an inorganic material, such as black plastic and landscaping fabric.

overwintering Growing plants indoors during winter.

perennial A plant that has a life span of more than two years.

pH A measure of the alkalinity or acidity of soil based on a scale of 1 (strongly acid) to 14 (strongly alkaline).

potpourri Long-lasting, fragrant mixtures of dried herbs and other crushed plant material.

poultice A paste made of minced, dried or fresh herbs, oatmeal and hot water. A poultice is used directly on the skin to draw out infection and relieve muscle aches.

propagate To reproduce a plant.

rhizome The underground runner or stem of a plant.

stool layering The propagation of a plant by mounding soil over the base of the parent plant; after four to six weeks, the new plants are removed and replanted.

taproot The strong, tapering central root of a plant that grows straight down in search of water and nutrients.

tincture An extract of an herb made by soaking the dried plant in alcohol for six weeks. Tinctures are much more concentrated and their potency lasts longer than decoctions or infusions.

topography The lay of an area of land, such as hills, valleys and slopes.

tussie-mussies Miniature herbal bouquets used to communicate sentiments.

MEASUREMENTS
1 teaspoon ¼ fl oz (5 ml)
1 tablespoon ½ fl oz (20 ml)
1 cup 8 fl oz (250 ml)
2½ cups 1 pint (600 ml)

INDEX

Entries in *italics* indicate illustrations and photos.

A

Achillea millefolium 93, 262–3, *263*
Agastache foeniculum 86
Agrimonia eupatoria 86
Agrimony 45, 86
Allelopathy 70–1
Allium
    sativum 89, 154–5, *154–5*
    schoenoprasum 88, 128–9, *128–9*
Aloe 45, 86, 94–5, *95*, 273, 294
Aloe vera 86, 94–5, *95*
Aloysia triphylla 90, 182–3, *182–3*
Althaea officinalis 90, 190–1, *191*
Anethum graveolens 88, 142–3, *142*
Angelica 40, 45, 86, 96–7, *96–7*, 271, 273
Angelica archangelica 86, 96–7, *96–7*
Anise 41, 86, 98–9, *99*, 285
Anise hyssop 45, 86
Annuals 40–1, 56, 312
Anthriscus cerefolium 87, 124–5, *125*
Antiseptic herbs 174

Aphids 69
Arctium lappa 87
Arctostaphylos uva-ursi 86
Armoracia rusticana 89, 168–9, *169*
Arnica 45, 86, 100–1, *100*, 294
Arnica montana 86, 100–1, *100*
Aromatherapy 292–3
Aromatic herbs 116, 148, 157, 158, 166, 169, 172
Artemisia
    abrotanum 93, 240–1, *241*
    absinthium 93, 260–1, *260–1*
    dracunculus 93, 248–9, *248–9*
    vulgaris 91
Aster yellows disease 65
Attraction plants 69, 122, 143, 151, 156, 163, 166, 172, 228, 246, 263

B

Barberry 45, 86, 294
Basil *13*, 40, 41, 52, 68, 83, 86, 102–5, *102–5*, 273, 306
Bathing, herbal 274–5

Bay 45, *75*, 86, 106–7, *106–7*, 273, 276
Bearberry 45, 86
Bee balm *see* bergamot
Beeswax 289
Beetles 60
Beginner herbs 53
Beneficial insects 60, 63, 69
Berberis vulgaris 86
Bergamot 45, 108–9, *108–9*, 273
Betony 45, 87
Betula spp. 87, 110–11, *110–11*
Biennials 42–3, 312
Birch 45, 87, 110–11, *110–11*
Blanching 83
Borage *12*, 41, 53, 74, 87, 112–13, *112–13*, 273
Borago officinalis 87, 112–13, *112–13*
Bouquet garni 300, 312
Brassica spp. 91, 196–7, *196–7*
Bulb *50*, 51
Bunches, hanging 79
Burdock 45, 87
Butter, herb 302–3

C

Calendula *41*, 52, 74, 87, 114–15,
    114–15, 294
Calendula officinalis 87, 114–15,
    114–15
Candlecraft 278–9
Capsicum annuum 87, 120–1, *121*
Caraway *42*, 74, 81, 87, 116–17, *117*
Carthamus tinctorius 92, 224–5, *225*
Carum carvi 87, 116–17, *117*
Cascara sagrada 45, 87
Catharanthus roseus 90
Catmint 45, 87, 118–19, *118*, 294
Cayenne pepper *41*, 87, 120–1, *121*
Ceanothus americanus 91
Chamaemelum nobile 87, 122–3, *122*
Chamomile 45, 53, 74, 87, 122–3,
    122, 273, 291, 294
    nature's nursemaid 67
Chemical release 70–1
Chervil 40, *41*, 83, 87, 124–5, *125*
Chicory 43, 45, 88, 126–7, *126–7*
Chimaphila umbellata 91, 212–13, *213*
Chives *14*, 45, 56, 75, 88, 128–9,
    128–9
    fungicidal tea 67

Chrysanthemum balsamita 88, 138–9,
    138–9
Cicely, sweet 40, 45, 93, 242–3,
    242–3
Cichorium intybus 88, 126–7, *126–7*
Citrus 276
Clary 45, 88, 130–1, *131*
Climate 12–15
Clover, red 92, 216–17, *216–17*
Coffea arabica 88, 132–3, *132*
Coffee 45, 88, 132–3, *132*
Coffee substitute 127, 141
Comfrey 45, 88, 134–5, *135*, 295
Companion plants *51*, 68–9, 71,
    129, 154, 156, 168, 199, 206,
    219, 229, 238, 247, 249, 250,
    253, 262
Complementary crops 69
Compost 24–7
Compress, herbal 288, 312
Cooking with herbs 300–1
Copper spray 66
Coriander 40, *41*, 81, 88, 136–7, *136*
Coriandrum sativum 88, 136–7, *136*
Cosmetic herbs 94, 114, 124, 150,
    164, 172, 183, 194, 258,
    274–5

Costmary 45, 88, 138–9, *138–9*
Crafts 267–81
    harvesting for 76–7
    herbs for craft use 124, 138,
        144,162
Creams and ointments 94, 97, 101,
    114, 150, 222
Crocus sativus 92, 226–7, *227*
Crop rotation 43
Cuttings 54–5, 312
Cymbopogon citratus 90, 180–1, *181*

D

Dandelion 45, 88, 140–1, *140–1*, 295
Decoction 286, 312
Design considerations 36–7
Diffuser 292
Dill *41*, *53*, 69, 71, 81, 83, 88,
    142–3, *142*, 273
Disease prevention 64–9
Diseased plants, disposal 65
Division 54, 312
Dock 45, 88, 144–5, *145*
Drying herbs 78–81, 108
    craft use, for 76–7
    dried arrangements 281
Dust removal 77

E

Elderflower, fungicidal tea 67
Elecampane 45, 88, 146–7, *146–7*
Equisetum spp. 89, 170–1, *170*
Essential oils 268–9, 275, 290–1
Eucalypts 45, 88, 148–9, *149*, 295

F

Fennel *15*, 41, 71, 83, 89, 150–1,
    151, 295
Fenugreek 41, 89, 152–3, *152*
Feverfew 45, 89
Fines herbes 312
Fixative 271, 312
Foeniculum vulgare 89, 150–1, *151*
Foliage 46–7
Forget-me-not 281
Freezing herbs 83
Fungicides 66–7
    organic *65*, 66

G

Galium
    odoratum 93, 244–5, *245*
    verum 90

Garlic 45, 68, 71, 89, 154–5, *154–5*,
    288, 295
    organic fungicide 65
    propagation *55*
Geranium, scented 45, *68*, 89,
    156–7, *156*, 273, 291
Germander 45, 53, 89, 158–9, *159*
Ginger 45, 89, 160–1, *160*
Ginseng root 285
Goldenrod 45, 89, 162–3, *163*, 281
Guide to medicinal herbs 294–7

H

Hamamelis virginiana 93, 258–9,
    258–9
Hand watering 16
Hardiness 52–3
    zone map 310–11, *311*
Harvesting
    crafts, for 76–7
    kitchen use, for 74–5
Herb bags 272–3
Herb health 59–71
Herbaceous perennials 45
Herbs, hostile 70–1
History of medicinal herbs 284–5

Homemade fungicides 66–7
Honey 289, 308
Hop 45, 89, 164–5, *164–5*, 295
Horehound *15*, 45, 89, 166–7, *166*,
    295
Horseradish 45, 89, 168–9, *169*
Horsetail 45, 89, 170–1, *170*
    fungicidal tea 67
Humulus lupulus 89, 164–5, *164–5*
Hyssop *15*, 45, 90, 172–3, *173*, 296
    nature's nursemaid 67
Hyssopus officinalis 90, 172–3, *173*

I

Identification 47
Indoor herbs 56–7
Infusion 286, 312
Insect repellents, herbal 276–7
Insect-repelling plants 129, 154, 175,
    179, 193, 199, 202, 237, 241
Insecticides 62–3, 261
Insects, beneficial 60, 63, 69
Interplanting 62
Inula helenium 88, 146–7, *146–7*
Iris 281
Iris x *germanica* 91, 204–5, *205*

K

Kitchen herbs 74–5, 299–309

L

Lady's bedstraw 45, 90
Laurus nobilis 86, 106–7, *106–7*
Lavandula angustifolia 90, 174–7, *175*
Lavender 44, 45, 53, 76, 77, 273,
    291, 308
    English 90, 174–7, *175*
    French *174, 176*
    Italian *177*
    oil 269
Lavender cotton 230–1, *231*
Layering 49, 51, 312
Leaves 46–9
Lemon balm 40, 45, 68, 90, 178–9,
    178–9
Lemon verbena 45, 90, 182–3,
    182–3
Lemongrass 45, 90, 180–1, *181*
Levisticum officinale 90, 184–5, *185*
Light exposure 18–19
    indoors 57
Lovage 45, *51*, 83, 90, 184–5, *185*

M

Madagascar periwinkle 90
Madder, dyer's 45, 90, 186–7, *187*
Map of hardiness zones 310–11, *311*
Marigold *41*, 70, 281
Marinade 306, 312
Marjoram 45, *52*, 83, 90, 188–9,
    188–9, 273
Marrubium vulgare 89, 166–7, *166*
Marsh mallow 45, 90, 190–1, *191*,
    296
Measurements 313
Medicinal herbs 282–97. *See also*
    Creams and ointments
    quick guide 294–7
Mediterranean herbs 53
Melissa officinalis 90, 178–9, *178–9*
Mentha
    pulegium 91, 210–11, *210–11*
    spp. 90, 192–5, *192–5*
Microwave drying 80
Mint *41*, 45, 68, *75*, 77, 83, 90,
    192–5, *192–5*, 287, 291, 297
Moisture 16–17
Monardo didyma 87, 108–9, *108–9*
Mugwort 45, 91

Mulch 28–9, 216, 313
Mustard 41, *52*, 91, 196–7, *196–7*
Myrrhis odorata 93, 242–3, *242–3*

N

Nasturtium *26*, 41, 42, 91, 198–9,
    198–9
Natural fungicides 67
Nepeta cataria 87, 118–19, *118*
Nettle 45, 91, 200–1, *200–1*
    tea 67, 200
New Jersey tea 45, 91
Nitrogen cycle 21, 26
Nutrients 22, 24

O

Ocimum basilicum 86, 102–5, *102–5*
Oil recipe 289, 306
Oils, essential 268–9, 275, 290–1
Ointment recipe 289
Ointments *see* Creams and ointments
Oregano 45, *80*, 91, 202–3, *203*
Organic fungicides 65, 66
Origanum
    majorana 90, 188–9, *188–9*
    vulgare 91, 202–3, *203*
Orris 45, 91, 204–5, *205*

Oven-drying 80, *81*
Overwintering 56, 313

P

Parsley 42–3, *43*, 71, 75, 83, 273, 296
  continental *207*
  curled 91, 206–7, *206–7*
  indoors 56, *56*
Passiflora incarnata 91, 208–9, *209*
Passionflower 45, 91, 208–9, *209*, 296
Patch planting 35, *35*
Paths 34, *34*
Pelargonium spp. 89, 156–7, *156*
Pennyroyal 45, 91, 210–11, *210–11*, 277
Peppermint *see* Mint
Perennials 44–5, 56, 313
Pest prevention 60–3, 185
Pet dip 277
Petals, drying 78
Petroselinum crispum 91, 206–7, *206–7*
pH of soil 23, 313
Pillows, herbal 272
Pimpinella anisum 86, 98–9, *99*

Pipsissewa 91, 212–13, *213*
Planning 31–7
Plantago major 91, 214–15, *215*
Plantain 41, 91, 214–15, *215*
Plaster, herbal 288
Potpourri 98, 106, 108, 116, 127, 130, 136, 156, 174, 204, 270–1, 313
Poultice 288, 313
Powdery mildew 66
Precautions 95, 97, 101, 113, 131, 135, 161, 171, 173, 201, 225, 233, 239, 245, 247, 253, 263, 287
Propagation 44, 54–5, 313

R

Rainfall 16–17
Recipes
  butter 303
  honey 308
  oil 289, 306
  ointment 289
  poultice 288
  salad dressings 306
  salt 307

  sweets 308–9
  syrup 289
  tincture 289
  vinegar 304
Red clover 45, 92, 216–17, *216–17*
Remedies, herbal 286–9
Rhamnus purshiana 87
Rhizome *50*, 313
Root herbs 74
Root systems 50–1
Rosa spp. 92, 220–1, *221*
Rose 45, 76, 92, 220–1, *221*, 281, 297, 308
  oil 268
Rosemary 45, 56, 75, 92, 218–19, *218–19*, 273, 277, 291, 297
Rosmarinus officinalis 92, 218–19, *218–19*
Rubia tinctorum 90, 186–7, *187*
Rue 92, 222–3, *223*
Rumex
  acetosa 92, 238–9, *238–9*
  crispus 88, 144–5, *145*
Rust spots *64*, 66
Ruta graveolens 92, 222–3, *223*

S

Sachets, herbal 273
Safflower 41, 92, 224–5, *225*
Saffron 45, 74, 92, 226–7, *227*
Sage 15, 45, 56, 70, 75, 92, 228–9, *228–9*, 273, 297
Salad dressings 306
Salt, herb 307
Salvia
   officinalis 92, 228–9, *228–9*
   sclarea 88, 130–1, *131*
Santolina 45, 92, 230–1, *231*
Santolina chamaecyparissus 92, 230–1, *231*
Saponaria officinalis 92, 236–7, *237*
Sassafras 19, 45, 92, 232–3, *233*
Sassafras albidum 92, 232–3, *233*
Satureja montana 92, 234–5, *235*
Savory, winter 45, 92, 234–5, *235*
Scientific names 86–93
Screens for drying 80, *81*
Seeds
   drying 81
   growing herbs for 74
Site considerations 32–3
Size considerations 34–5

Snails 61
Soap, herbal 274–5
Soapwort 45, 92, 236–7, *237*
Soil 20–3
Solidago spp. 89, 162–3, *163*
Sorrel 45, 75, 92, 238–9, *238–9*
Southernwood 76, 93, 240–1, *241*, 273
Stachys officinalis 87
Stems 48–9
Stool layering 313
Storing 82–3
Style considerations 36–7
Sulfur spray 66
Sunlight exposure 18–19, 57
Sweet cicely 40, 45, 93, 242–3, *242–3*
Sweet woodruff 45, 93, 244–5, *245*
Sweets, herbal 308–9
Symphytum officinale 88, 134–5, *135*
Syrup recipe 289

T

Tanacetum
   parthenium 89
   vulgare 93, 246–7, *246–7*
Tansy 45, 93, 246–7, *246–7*

Taproot 50, 313
Taraxacum officinale 88, 140–1, *140–1*
Tarragon 45, 83, 93, 248–9, *248–9*, 273, 306
Tea herbs 96, 108, 110, 122, 152, 286–7
Teucrium chamaedrys 89, 158–9, *159*
Thyme 45, 53, 68, 75, 80, 83, 93, 250–1, *250*, 273, 297
Thymus vulgaris 93, 250–1, *250*
Tincture 289, 313
Topography 313
Trifolium pratense 92, 216–17, *216–17*
Trigonella foenum–graecum 89, 152–3, *152*
Tropaeolum majus 91, 198–9, *198–9*
Tussie-mussie 280–1, *280*, 313

U

Urtica dioica 91, 200–1, *200–1*

V

Valerian 45, 93, 252–3, *252–3*, 297
Valeriana officinalis 93, 252–3, *252–3*
Verbena officinalis 93, 254–5, *255*
Vervain 41, 93, 254–5, *255*
Vinegar, herbal 304–5

Viola odorata 93, 256–7, *256–7*
Violet 45, 93, 256–7, *256–7*, 281, *281*

W

Warnings 95, 97, 101, 113, 131, 135, 161, 171, 173, 201, 225, 233, 239, 245, 247, 253, 263, 287

Washing herbs 77
Weed prevention 28
Windy conditions 19
Winter herbs 13
Witch hazel 45, 93, 258–9, *258–9*, 297
Woodruff, sweet 93, 244–5, *245*
Woody perennials 45
Wormwood *70*, 93, 260–1, *260–1*

Wreath, herbal 281

Y

Yarrow 45, 76, 77, 93, 262–3, *263*, 281, 297

Z

Zingiber officinale 89, 160–1, *160*
Zinnia 281

ACKNOWLEDGMENTS

Weldon Owen would like to thank the following people: Sarah Anderson, Lisa Boehm, Trudie Craig, Peta Gorman, Michael Hann, Aliza Pinczewski, Puddingburn Publishing Services (index)

TEXT Bonnie Lee Appleton, C. Colston Burrell, Susan McClure, Patricia S. Michalak, Nancy J. Ondra, Rob Proctor, Sally Roth, Alfred F. Schneider, Elizabeth Stell

ILLUSTRATIONS Susanna Addario, Martin Camm, Mike Gorman, Stuart McVicar, David Mackay, David Moore, Barbara Rodanska, Claudia Saraceni, Sharif Tarabay

PHOTOGRAPHS Ad-Libitum/Stuart Bowey & Steve Trevaskis; Heather Angel; Ardea, London: A. P. Patterson; Auscape/Jacana: Paul Nief; A–Z Botanical Collection; Gillian Beckett; Bruce Coleman Ltd: B & C Calhoun, Eric Crichton, Gerald Cubitt, Rocco Longo, Hans Reinhard, Michel Viard; John Callanan; John Hollingshead; Corel Corporation; Denise Craig; Thomas Eltzroth; Rowan Fotheringham; The Garden Picture Library: Brian Carter, Gary Rogers, Mel Watson; Harry Smith Collection; Stirling Macoboy; Cheryl Maddocks; Kylie Mulquin; Clive Nichols; Photos Horticultural; G. R. "Dick" Roberts; Rodale Stock Images; Tony Rodd; Lorna Rose; Chris Shorten; S & O Matthews; David Wallace; Weldon Trannies

CONSULTANT EDITOR Geoffrey Burnie has 20 years' experience in horticulture. He is the author of several books on gardening and has been a consultant and contributor to *Better Homes and Gardens* magazine since 1983.